ECONOMIC HISTORY REVIEW SUPPLEMENT

5

R. H. TAWNEY'S COMMONPLACE BOOK

too weak, but because it is too strong, not for the sake of the State, but for the sake of itself. Its position is defined in the words "He that is greatest among you let him be the servant of all". The church cannot help being powerful: but it can help trusting the arm of the flesh. It must be free to be a servant. The ancient question whether church is to be above State or state is to be above church finds its solution in a free church resigning the temporalities for the sake of the spiritualities.

December 11th. I see Wells is writing in some magazine a paper on what the world will be when science has trebled our wealth. It is astonishing how people can go on believing in the face of all the evidence that society can be improved by spilling its strength, by adding one to one. It never has been & never will be, because the social problem is one of proportion not of magnitudes. Conversely I am not much perturbed by the question what will happen to great Britain when she has exhausted her coal, or when other countries

R. H. Tawney's Commonplace Book

EDITED AND
WITH AN INTRODUCTION BY
J. M. WINTER and D. M. JOSLIN

ECONOMIC HISTORY REVIEW
SUPPLEMENT
5

CAMBRIDGE
AT THE UNIVERSITY PRESS
1972

Published by the Syndics of the Cambridge University Press
Bentley House, 200 Euston Road, London NW1 2DB
American Branch: 32 East 57th Street, New York, N.Y.10022

© Economic History Society 1972

Library of Congress Catalogue Card Number: 71–164454

ISBN: 0 521 08313 3

Printed in Great Britain
by W & J Mackay Ltd, Chatham

CONTENTS

EDITORIAL NOTE

THIS transcription and annotation of R. H. Tawney's
Commonplace Book was made by Dr J. M. Winter in collabora-
tion with the late Professor D. M. Joslin. The introduction is a
joint draft to which it had been intended that Professor Joslin
should add certain further material. His sudden and tragic
death in October 1970 came before this task could be
completed. Dr Winter had meanwhile taken up a post at the
Hebrew University Jerusalem. In order to avoid delay, the
decision was taken, in consultation with the editors of the
Economic History Review acting on behalf of the Economic
History Society, to prepare the work for publication as quickly
as possible, and also to add the short appreciation of Professor
Joslin which follows this note. The editorial work in preparing
the Commonplace Book for the press has been done by
Professor D. C. Coleman; and the appreciation of David
Joslin is by Professor M. M. Postan.

As far as possible the arrangement, spelling, and punctuation
of the original Commonplace Book have been retained. Because,
however, it was kept essentially for private purposes, it proved
necessary to introduce a certain amount of consistency and
rationalization in such matters as punctuation and the
rendering of dates. Apart from these changes all editorial
insertions or interpretations are shown thus [ ]; where there is
any doubt about a missing or illegible word, thus [?]. Some

entries in the original appear not to have been made in strictly chronological order. This seems sometimes to have been because blank pages were left and subsequently filled in or because entries for a slightly earlier date were added as afterthoughts. There are only a very few such examples and in order to preserve continuity for the reader all entries have been put in chronological order.

The place of publication of works cited in the footnotes is London unless otherwise stated.

The Commonplace Book is in the possession of Mr J. M. K. Vyvyan, nephew and literary executor of the late Professor Tawney. The editors wish to express their thanks to Mr Vyvyan for permission to prepare this edition. Much help was also rendered by the late Sir Richard Rees in making the original transcription.

D. M. JOSLIN
1925–1970

In age, upbringing and character, as well as in the nature of
their studies, David Joslin and R. H. Tawney were very different
men. Although Tawney's historical work was based on much
detailed research it was to a remarkable extent dependent on
inspired guesses and flashes of insight and was deeply coloured
by his likes and dislikes. Joslin's work on the other hand was
highly rational and matter-of-fact. His very choice of a first
subject for research – eighteenth-century banking – was
prompted by an interest in the origins and processes of
industrialization and economic growth: an interest Tawney
never completely acquired and for which he even felt a certain
amount of moral distaste. Similarly, Joslin's later switch to
Latin American history was very un-Tawney-like in its detachment from the intense Englishness of most of Tawney's
interests and preoccupations. For all his socialist views and
humble personal tastes Tawney preserved throughout his life
the outward manners – not only the tone of voice, but also the
façon d'agir – of an Edwardian and even Victorian gentleman
with family roots in the English countryside, the Church, and
the Indian Civil Service. On the other hand, Joslin's early life
has to be seen against the background of the inter-war and
post-war meritocracy.

Tawney had grown into what he eventually became by
rejecting all he owed to, or could blame on, the education in a
great public school and the young gentleman's milieu in

pre-1914 Oxford. David Maelgwyn Joslin was Welsh and
Welsh-speaking, born the son of a schoolmaster in Barry,
Glamorgan. Barry Grammar School, a scholarship at St John's
College, Cambridge, wartime service in naval intelligence, a
fellowship at Pembroke and, in 1965, the chair of Economic
History at Cambridge: these were the successive steps of his
professional career. Both men had many friends and very few
enemies; yet superficially their attitudes were greatly
dissimilar. Tawney was no respecter of fools; he could be
direct, even scathing, in his personal reactions. When re-
proached for being a 'tart' Christian his reply was that our
Lord's injunction was to love our fellow human beings and not
necessarily to like them. On the other hand, Joslin always
appeared to be conscious of other people's susceptibilities and
anxious not to trespass and not to hurt. This made him an ideal
committee man, an indispensable member of the administrative
democracy of his university and college, an ideal sponsor of
projects and a highly sympathetic channel of communication.

Joslin's way to goodness was costlier than Tawney's. If by
the end of his short life he had completed so few of the
scholarly projects on which he was engaged, this was largely
due to the time and energy he gave to other people; above all to
his administrative duties, both for his college – he had been
Senior Tutor at Pembroke before his election to the chair of
Economic History – and for the university, on the Faculty
Board of History and on the General Board of the Faculties.
Earlier still he had laboured many long hours as assistant editor
of the *Economic History Review* and later as joint editor of the
Cambridge Economic History of Europe. He was instrumental in
beginning the series of Cambridge Latin American Studies as

well as launching the new *Journal of Latin American Studies,* of which he was joint editor. These tasks he did, not because he sought distraction from his scholarly work, but out of a deep interest in his varied subjects and a concern for the university where he spent most of his life.

To this extent some of the differences between the two men were more superficial than real. Like Tawney, Joslin devoted to men and causes the time and the energy he could ill spare. Tawney's causes were more, so to speak, general: the Labour Party, the W.E.A., social work in settlements. Joslin's were more directly related to the bodies to which he belonged and to the offices he held. They did not, at first sight, appear to entail any ideological and moral commitments. Yet those who knew him were left in no doubt about his humanity, the emotional as well as intellectual springs of his work, and the pleasure he derived from it. Of these qualities there could be no better proof than the work he did with Dr Winter for Tawney's Commonplace Book at a time when his other obligations were at their heaviest.

M. M. POSTAN

INTRODUCTION

R. H. TAWNEY was a man of deep Christian beliefs and
powerful emotions, and nowhere can we gain as full a view of
his mind and temperament, of the limitations of his ideas as
well as their strengths, as in the Commonplace Book or diary
which he kept at Manchester from 1912 to 1914. This document
is a unique record of the assumptions which supported
Tawney's lifelong work as a socialist and as a scholar. The
pattern of his historical interests and, in embryonic form, the
outline of many of the arguments which he later developed in
his three most influential books. *The Acquisitive Society* (1921),
Religion and the Rise of Capitalism (1926), and *Equality* (1931),
clearly emerge from the pages of this pre-war diary.

There is no contemporary equivalent to the Commonplace
Book. Beatrice Webb's diaries are an invaluable record of the
issues and personalities of the labour movement, but the
reflective passages – even her periodic ventures into meta-
physics – were different from Tawney's in style and purpose.
Beatrice Webb wrote for future readers, in the well-founded
belief that what she had to say would be of interest to later
generations. In fact she spent a good deal of time in 1918
editing her diaries and inserting helpful introductory notes
and commentaries on the text for her anticipated audience. The
Commonplace Book, on the other hand, was not written for publication. It is above all a private document, a record of the personal
concerns which Tawney rarely, if ever, confided or shared with

his contemporaries in his correspondence and other writings.

Tawney appears in the pages of this diary as an isolated man, engaged in an exploration of the internal world of his Christian beliefs. Yet the amorphous design and idiosyncratic construction of the Commonplace Book contribute greatly to its intellectual coherence and forcefulness. Without an audience, which more likely than not would have been composed of people who did not share his religious frame of mind, Tawney achieved in this diary a clarity and simplicity of style seldom equalled in his later work. There are none of the intricate allusions or the heaviness of rhetoric which give to his later prose its character-istic flavour of elaborate and elegant irony. Instead he wrote his diary directly and unselfconsciously in an introspective dia-logue with what he called the voice of conscience within him. In one of the early entries in the diary, Tawney provided a clue as to why he had begun it at this particular time and in this particular form. On 26 October 1912, he noted that

The secret of growth is self-surrender, and as much so in matters of intellect as in matter of morals. If a man wants to do serious scientific work in any sphere, he must become impersonal, suppress his own fancies and predilections, and try and listen to reason speaking within him.

The Commonplace Book was the result of Tawney's attempt to articulate that voice of reason or, in his terms, that voice of Christian morality, and to follow its guidance in the construction of an outline of his life's work as an historian and social critic.

By 1912, at the age of thirty-two, Tawney had come to enjoy a measure of stability and contentment in his professional work as a writer and teacher.[1] After Balliol and Toynbee Hall, he

[1] Biographical details may be found in: T. S. Ashton, 'Richard Henry Tawney 1880–1962', *Proceedings of the British Academy* (1962), pp. 461–82; J. R. Williams, R. M. Titmuss and F. J. Fisher, *R. H. Tawney: A Portrait by Several Hands* (1960); J. M. Winter, 'R. H. Tawney's early political thought', *Past and Present* (May 1970), 71–96.

had been fortunate enough to have found in the Workers' Educational Association (W.E.A.) a way to combine effectively his political and scholarly interests with his moral commitments. In the years prior to the First World War, he lived in Manchester whence he could travel to parts of Lancashire and the Potteries to teach in the various university tutorial classes with which he had been associated since their inception in 1908. Many of his friends and companions were students or fellow tutors for the W.E.A. as the Commonplace Book shows.[1] Tawney then was also able to join the circle of students drawn to George Unwin, professor of economic history at the University of Manchester. Unwin's personal influence was warmly acknowledged in Tawney's introductory memoir to Unwin's collected papers, published posthumously in 1927.

In 1912, Tawney had also been appointed director of the Ratan Tata Foundation, which was affiliated to the London School of Economics and established to conduct research on poverty and related industrial problems. His first project was to examine the effects of legislation which had set up trade boards to fix minimum wage-rates for poorly-organized trades. In addition, when Tawney started to keep his diary in the spring in 1912, he had just completed his first full-length historical study, *The Agrarian Problem in the Sixteenth Century*.

[1] On Tawney's contribution to the extension of university education to the working class, see the journal of the W.E.A., *Highway*, which listed annually all tutorial classes, and *Oxford and Working-class Education* (1908), which was the report of the joint committee of university and working-class representatives on the relation of the university 'to the Higher Education of Workpeople'. Among the members of this committee who are mentioned in the Commonplace Book were T. B. Strong, the dean of Christ Church, A. L. Smith of Balliol, and Sidney Ball of St John's College. Two flattering references to Tawney's classes at Longton and Rochdale in 1908 are cited in the report as evidence of the potential value of extension education.

The time had come for him to consider the path of his future research as well as the assumptions which he brought and would continue to bring to his 'serious scientific work'.

Contemporary events provided Tawney with another compelling reason to begin an examination of his political and historical ideas. During the years 1911–12, there occurred the outbreak of the greatest series of industrial disputes in Britain since 1889–90. First the dockers, then the railwaymen, then the miners struck in turn, and their actions seemed part of a pattern of discontent which contemporaries named 'the labour unrest'. By chance, on the day of Tawney's first entry in the Commonplace Book, 19 April 1912, the aggressive union leader Tom Mann was arrested for seditious writing during the national coal strike, which had ended a fortnight before. In March 1912, Mann had spoken in Salford to denounce the presence of troops in Manchester and had urged soldiers not to fire on strikers. Publishing this plea had brought him a six-month jail sentence. His act and its consequences in a sense symbolized both the renewed spirit of militancy in the trade-union movement and the reaction of fear and apprehension which the strikes evoked in governing circles at the time. By mid-1912 there was little reason to conclude, as was the case, that the peak of strike activity had passed. What seemed far more likely then was the continuation and intensification of industrial conflict and the bitterness and hardship it inevitably generated.[1]

---

[1] On the labour unrest, see E. H. Phelps Brown, *The Growth of British Industrial Relations* (1959); G. Dangerfield, *The Strange Death of Liberal England* (1936); H. Pelling, *Popular Politics and Society in Late Victorian Britain* (1968), ch. 9; W. H. B. Court, *Scarcity and Choice in History* (Cambridge, 1970), ch. 2.

The causes and consequences of the labour unrest were
urgent questions which commanded the attention of Tawney
and every other man who thought seriously about political and
social issues in the pre-war years. Socialists in particular felt
compelled to take account of the new situation; and, at this
time, many admitted the need to examine and if necessary to
revise their political ideas or tactics.

Beatrice and Sidney Webb were among the first to recognize
the importance of a restatement of socialist thought before the
outbreak of the First World War. Consequently they wrote a
series of articles entitled 'What is Socialism?' to help launch
their journalistic venture, the *New Statesman*, in 1913. In
addition they organized through the Fabian Society a committee
of inquiry on the control of industry, in an attempt to remedy
the Fabians' relative silence on the questions of the relations of
production and workers' control, issues which had been
brought to the fore by the labour unrest. These articles and
reports contain a complete exposition of the Webbs'
collectivist or state socialist ideas, which served as the main
point of departure for the views of all British socialists,
including Tawney.

Those who were already hostile to the Webbs' ideas saw in
the strike wave confirmation of their views that the old Fabian
methods and theory had failed, and that a fresh approach in
socialist strategy was therefore urgently needed. One group
that attempted to meet this problem were the guild socialists,
who emphatically rejected the views of the Webbs and all those
who stressed political action. Instead they advocated a
policy of militant industrial action which, they believed, would
lead ultimately to a partnership in the control of the economy

between the state, representing the consumers, and the trade unions, organized on national and industrial lines in professional bodies called 'guilds' which would represent the producers. Their aim was to develop a hybrid position, composed of parts of collectivist doctrine, without its worship of the state, and parts of syndicalist thought, without its complete denial of political authority.

Although Tawney did not subscribe to guild socialism at this time,[1] he did agree that the old Fabian theory was outdated and in need of serious revision. Despite his passive membership of the Fabian Society since 1906 and the Independent Labour Party since 1909, Tawney's deep scepticism about the tactics and overall strategy of Parliamentary socialism is clearly seen in his pre-war diary.

It is in this context of the re-appraisal of British socialist thought as a direct result of the labour unrest that R. H. Tawney's Commonplace Book must be read. His comments and reflections show that he shared with his socialist contemporaries a number of basic premises. What they held in common was the belief that while the strikes had revealed a powerful

---

[1] Parts of *The Acquisitive Society* reflect Tawney's acceptance of certain guild socialist ideas after the First World War. See also this statement in a speech by Tawney in the early 1920s: 'Whether our [economic] reorganisation is an advance or a reaction will depend on the clearness of our analysis of the present situation, and on the programme with which we meet it. Though possibly an unorthodox Gild Socialist, and certainly disagreeing with some of its exponents, I welcome it both for the one and the other...I welcome the gild movement, therefore, in the first place because it brings English socialism out of the back waters and bypaths of government regulation, in which it was boring itself ten years ago, into the mainstream of the Socialist tradition, which has as its object not merely the alleviation of poverty, but an attack on the theory of functionless property.' – 'Speeches on various occasions', Tawney Papers, British Library of Political and Economic Science, London School of Economics.

current of discontent among large sections of the organized working class, nevertheless the labour movement was crippled and would remain crippled so long as it lacked a focus and guiding force in a coherent political philosophy, the creation of which was the primary intellectual task of the day.

Tawney's contribution to that effort in the pre-war years was distinctive, though incomplete. His Christian faith and idealist's outlook, stated with simplicity in the Commonplace Book, led him to construct the outline of a socialist position fundamentally at odds with the views both of the 'old guard' Fabians and of the guildsmen. Tawney could not accept either school of thought at this time because, in his opinion, they were equally obsessed with issues of structure and administration in politics or industry. They both overlooked, therefore, what Tawney took to be fundamental, that is, that institutional changes on any level were superficial unless they were based on a prior shift in the assumptions which men brought to all human associations. Without such an alteration in the moral notions, the standards of conduct which, he held, guided the actions of men in their daily lives, Tawney predicted that the contemporary pattern of domination and exploitation would reappear, regardless of the future form of social organization. How such spiritual changes were to come about was not at all clear from his pre-war writing, but his lifelong dedication to educational work was at least a personal response to the problem.

The Commonplace Book also demonstrates the way Tawney brought to the study of economic history the same assumptions which underlay his critique of social thought. His central concern in both cases was to deepen the discussion of economic issues by reference to the ethical dilemmas which, he believed, have always accompanied the attempts men have made to organize the production of wealth.

This view of history as a branch of moral philosophy is one of the most salient features of his writings. It determined the subjects he chose to study and the angle of attack he pursued in his research. It accounts both for the powerful impact of his work on a generation which shared his interests as well as its rejection by scholars who value objectivity above all and who see in present-mindedness an invitation to distortion.[1] Few men today would subscribe to Tawney's conviction, stated in the preface to *The Agrarian Problem*, that

> The supreme interest of economic history lies, it seems to me, in the clue which it offers to the development of those dimly conceived presuppositions as to social expediency which influence the actions not only of statesmen, but of humble individuals and classes, and influence, perhaps, most decisively those who are least conscious of any theoretical bias.[2]

Fewer still would share his hostility to the position, which he identified in the Commonplace Book with the name of Alfred Marshall, that economic questions had to be approached with scientific detachment. Nothing could be further from Tawney's attitude, which took the act of moral judgment to be central to the historian's task.

The essential unity of his work and thought is reflected finally in the circumstances which brought about the termination of the Commonplace Book. The last entry is dated 28 December 1914, about one month after Tawney had volun-

[1] For a spirited statement of this position, see Professor G. R. Elton's inaugural lecture, *The Future of the Past* (Cambridge, 1969).
[2] *The Agrarian Problem in the Sixteenth Century* (1912), p. vii.

teered for service with the British Army as a private, but before
he reported for active duty. The decision to enlist was perfectly
consistent with his religious and political beliefs. Tawney's
war was primarily a struggle between ideas which at certain
times, such as during the German invasion of Belgium, were
personified as nations. Germany thus became a metaphor for
political evil, which was dangerous and to be opposed
precisely because its spirit was so contagious. Armed resistance
to Prussian militarism was therefore a continuation on another
level of the struggle against the mechanical oppression and
exploitation which Tawney found so repugnant in British
industrial society, and which he tried to combat in one way or
another throughout his life.

Once he had worked out his commitment to the Allied
cause, the interruption of his work and the potential danger
seemed relatively unimportant. If the place of the Christian in
peace-time was, as Tawney believed, at the forefront of the
burning social issues of the day, so it followed that the place of
the Christian during war was also at the front and among the
men in the ranks. And with these convictions Tawney went
off to fight. Eighteen months later, on the first day of the Battle
of the Somme, Tawney was severely wounded. After a period
of recuperation and reflection on the consequences of his
ordeal, he gradually returned to the political and historical
work which he had outlined in the Commonplace Book.

The structure of Tawney's beliefs was strong enough to
withstand the tests of war and its aftermath. He experienced
little of the disillusionment and withdrawal as a result of
misplaced hopes or false expectations which so many other
socialists suffered at this time. Nor did he flirt with communism

as the harbinger of a new age. Tawney needed no ideological re-orientation after the war because his fundamental position had remained unshaken. It is not surprising, therefore, that Tawney kept no Commonplace Book after the First World War. He had already made up his mind on the moral questions which dominated his life's work.

On another level, however, Tawney's war experience was formative. The fact that the nation virtually with one voice had committed its material and human resources to the prosecution of a just cause convinced him that the conflict had altered the internal development of British political and social affairs in a positive way. He saw in the national mobilization for war the faint outline of a future stable society in which men were bound together for the moral and physical betterment of all. This spiritual unity which the Allied cause generated in its first months fulfilled what Tawney defined as the necessary precondition for institutional action. He believed that all political associations are inherently mechanical bodies, capable of effective action only when animated by ideas which exist outside and grow independently of them. Tawney was convinced that the First World War had uncovered and developed such a progressive movement in mass political and social attitudes. Accordingly, during the war he adjusted his tactical views and began to work actively within the reconstructed Labour Party.

Tawney stood unsuccessfully at Rochdale as the I.L.P. candidate during the 'khaki election' of 1918. His talents were probably better directed in his work as the chief formulator of the party's educational policy in its newly-formed educational advisory committee.

Reform of the Anglican Church was another subject raised
in the Commonplace Book to which Tawney devoted his
attention in the last years of the war. While recuperating from
his war wounds in 1916, he joined the bishop of Oxford,
Charles Gore, and numerous other distinguished churchmen
in preparing a report which was published two years later as
Christianity and Industrial Problems. The extension of many of
the arguments Tawney raised in his pre-war diary may be
found in this remarkable document. At the same time, he joined
his friend and contemporary at Rugby and Balliol, William
Temple, then rector of St James, Piccadilly, in organizing the
'Life and Liberty Movement', which was dedicated to
securing freedom of action for the Church so that it could
contribute to the anticipated restructuring of social life at the
end of the war.

In the decade following the armistice, Tawney continued to
develop many of the ideas which he had first formulated in
the Commonplace Book. His experience as a member of the
Sankey Commission on the Coal Industry in 1919 deepened his
critique of economic privilege, which he then expounded in
various pamphlets and in an article for the *Hibbert Journal*,
which was later published in expanded form as *The Acquisitive
Society*. In 1922 he delivered the Scott Holland Memorial
Lectures at King's College, London, in which he developed
the possibilities inherent in the simple question he had phrased
a decade earlier in the Commonplace Book and without the
assistance of Max Weber: 'I wonder if Puritanism produced
any special attitude toward economic matters.' Four years
later these lectures were published as *Religion and the Rise of
Capitalism*. The effect of this book on both social and historical

thought in Britain was profound.[1] Three years later an invitation to deliver the Halley Stewart Lectures allowed him to extend the exposition of his pre-war ideas about the 'religion of inequality' and the resultant status relationships which sustained and perpetuated capitalism. When *Equality* appeared two years later, Tawney's creative contribution to British socialist thought, which was prefigured in the Commonplace Book, had been completed.

J. M. WINTER

Pembroke College, Cambridge   D. M. JOSLIN
18 August 1970

---

[1] For example, see Professor Court's statement in his moving essay 'Growing up in an age of anxiety', in *Scarcity and Choice in History*, pp. 17–18: 'It is difficult at this distance of time to make clear to those who never knew him or who never read his books when they were written the exceptional position held by Richard Henry Tawney in scholarship and politics in the twenties... He occupied as an historian a position half-way between politics and philosophy. This made him extremely interesting to young people trying to make up their own minds...But in the quiet of the late twenties it was still possible to read Tawney's book [*Religion and the Rise of Capitalism*] and to be impressed by the power of his argument, especially if one was disposed to be critical of society as I was. The effect with me was to make me think seriously for the first time about doing historical research.' Indeed, even those historians who find Tawney's influence pernicious do not deny the impact of his work.

THE TEXT OF
THE COMMONPLACE BOOK

If found, please return to R. H. Tawney, 24 Shakespeare Street,
C-on-M,[1] Manchester.
PRIVATE.

1912

19 April. J. ELKIN[2] (on a proposal that the Longton, Hanley
and Stoke classes should affiliate to the W.E.A.): 'I want to
support this proposal. This society is going to have a great
deal to do with the education of the workers, especially in
teaching economics and industrial history, and the workers
ought to see that there [*sic*] point of view receives attention.
We know how some of these people teach industrial history,
that governments have always been moved by a kind consideration for the people, and that people are poor through their own
fault. We've heard of them talk this at Oxford. The truth is
that through the ages the workers have been bottom dog, and
we've got to see that the education given is of a kind to make
them realize that.' (not exact words, but substance)

MYSELF: 'Any of you read *Seems so?*[3] Its main idea seems to
be that working classes hate interference of rich – inspectors,
visitors, and so on in their affairs.'

E. HOBSON:[4] 'Well they did hate the Health Visitors here at
first, especially when they were single women. But they seem
to welcome them now. It's a matter of habit. But the grievance
is that inspection and so on does not press upon every one

---

1 Chorlton-on-Medlock.
2 John Elkin, a miner and student in Tawney's Longton tutorial class.
3 Stephen Reynolds, and Bob and Tom Woolley, *Seems So! A Working-Class
   View of Politics* (1912).
4 Edmund Hobson, a colliery weighman and student in Tawney's Longton
   tutorial class.

equally. No inspector thinks of going into houses in —— road. When I was at the elementary school the attendance officer would come round if I missed a day. When I went to the secondary school, no one bothered about it. People dislike that sort of interference, because it's applied to one class and not to another.'

ELKIN: 'It's the way in which they make us ignorant people live in the way they think we ought.'

20 April. What's the cause of the labour unrest?

[?HARTE]:[1] 'More wages. Prices have gone up. There's four shillings less purchasing power in the sovereign since the Boer War. The screws [have] been turned so far that people have begun to realize it.'

'But prices have been going up since 1896.'

'Yes, but profits have gone up enormously without wages rising, and the workers have begun to find it out. Then there has been the influence of Tom Mann. His personality can hold a crowd of 5000 labourers and make them act as one. One of the causes of trouble is that people who manage businesses don't pay enough attention to them. Take the case of Rileys[2] (a firm): any one who knew the trade could see that there was waste in the business. They didn't understand the way to do things. But they were hard up through gambling in stocks and shares, and so they cut wages.'

'What was the truth about the textile dispute?'

'The trouble rose about the other Riley. Riley had been on

---

[1] This name is obscure in the text; possibly A. E. Harte, author of 'Economic science and social evolution', *Economic Review*, XXI (April 1911), 175–86.
[2] Probably A. Riley & Co. Ltd, Manchester cotton manufacturers.

the ctee of the local weavers' union. He had had trouble with the firm where he worked. He was a bad weaver, and the firm had told him he must go on to 3 looms instead of 4 or leave. He left and claimed victimization pay from the union. The union refused it on the ground that he was a bad weaver.'

'Is it a wise policy striking shops in order to get everyone into the union?'

'Sometimes. The weavers didn't win in the last dispute. But they weren't beaten. The employers began by claiming to have an absolutely free hand in the selection of men. But they withdrew that claim later.'

ANOTHER SPEAKER: 'The difficulty is that there is no equality in bargaining between a firm and a worker – the firm stands to lose interest on its capital, the worker to starve, and so he can't wait.'

Class-ethics are a most curious thing. It is the ineradicable assumption of the upper classes that a workman should be primarily a good productive tool. He is always judged from this point of view, from the assumption that all he wants or ought to want, is not to live but to work. The slightest extravagance in him is condemned by the very people who, even though far from wealthy according to modern standards, never dream of denying themselves small pleasure and luxuries. What does 'a workman' want with theatres, or books, or time to himself? The education of his children is treated in the same fashion. L.E.A.s economize on elementary schools in order to spend money on secondary education. The Boards' regulations say that in secondary schools the air space per child must be 17 ft., in elementary schools 11 ft. and the Lancashire C.C. has many schools where it is only 8 sq. ft. Every secondary school must have a playground of at least 4 acres. $\frac{1}{4}$ acre is thought enough for many elementary schools. The workman is supposed to practise a rigid economy. If he is even slightly self-indulgent, he is told that it is 'his own fault' when he gets into difficulties, and there is no sympathy for him accordingly. He is not regarded as a human being, who wants [to] live, but as so much power that is bought in the market, like electricity or gas. And for ages he has acquiesced in this attitude himself. The new thing is that now he means to *live* not only to labour.

21 April. The middle and upper class view in social reform is that it should regulate the worker's *life* in order that he may *work* better. The working class view of economic reform is that it should regulate his *work*, in order that he may have a chance of living. Hence to working people licensing reform, insurance acts, etc. seems beginning at the wrong end. 'Give us a fair chance' they say 'and all this [?humbug] will be unnecessary.'

Plan of a book – 'Economic Privilege and Economic Liberty'
Chapter I. In all European countries the 19th century began with 2 demands (a) for economic liberty (b) for the abolition of privilege. Thus

    (i)   in France this was the note of the Revolution –
           Rousseau: the abolition of feudal privileges etc.
    (ii) in Prussia the absolutist government threw itself on
           the same side in matters of detail.
    (iii) It was the keynote of the radical and individualist
           movement in England.

Chapter II. The working of this idea out in 'practice'.

Chapter III. Disillusionment with it. Modern discontent presents at once an analogy to and a contrast with the the [*sic*] discontent which preceded the French Revolution. The discontent, though often said to be due to poverty, is not solely due to it.

Chapter IV. Detailed illustrations (a) Liberty and slavery.

Chapter V. Detailed illustrations (b) privilege.

29 April. G. LANSBURY (in House of Commons).[1] To a statement by me that the Labour Party ought to get and train its young men: 'I don't altogether agree: I'm very much afraid of taking them away from their work. They tend to become superior and "intellectual". I know it's difficult for them to do propaganda and other things without leisure. But they must fight it out somehow. I think the only "intellectual" in our party has not been good for it. I'm sure it would be much healthier if individual members had more initiative. The tendency now is always to ask "what do the officers say?" Or take a Sanders.[2] He is an excellent fellow. But he was taken up by wit and sent to study in foreign Universities, and one can't help feeling that he thinks he knows just how things should be done. Barnett[3]

[1] George Lansbury, at that time Labour M.P. for Bow and Bromley who resigned to stand on the issue of woman's suffrage and lost his seat in 1912; a former poor law commissioner from 1905 to 1909 who signed the minority report; shared Tawney's religious outlook and wrote and spoke with an evangelist's zeal.

[2] W. S. Sanders, Fabian socialist; secretary of the Fabian Society, 1914–20.

[3] S. A. Barnett, warden of Toynbee Hall from 1884 to 1906 where he guided many graduates into various forms of social work. He placed Tawney in the Children's Country Holiday Fund, where he met his future wife, Jeannette Beveridge, the sister of William Beveridge, a contemporary of Tawney at Balliol and another of Canon Barnett's protégés. Tawney contributed a chapter on Barnett's educational ideas to his wife's *Life* which appeared posthumously in 1919. (Dame Henrietta Octavia Barnett, *Canon Barnett: his life, work, and friends, by his wife* (2 vols., 1919).)

sent round a circular lately asking for opinions as to whether it wld be wise to train young workmen for the clergy. Webb and I said no.'

The strikes have done a lot of good. We were going to sleep and they woke us up. But the Labour Party in the House helped, for it prevented McKenna doing what was done by Winston Churchill when he was at the Home Office.[1] This has been a wonderful year. I think the cause of the unrest is mainly that the street corner preaching is at length beginning to have effect. And the Tories are right in saying that Lloyd George's speeches have contributed to it. A man who doesn't pay attention to a socialist orator is caught by the Chancellor of the Exchequer.

4 May. There are two fundamental questions of economics which must be answered before one can undertake an intelligent inquiry into the distribution of wealth. The first is: how far is poverty due to the inadequate natural resources of the country where men are poor? A peasant can't get more than a certain crop from a given field – a people can't get more than a certain crop from a given area of land. This involves a consideration of population and productive power.

The second question is this: For the last 100 years man's command over nature has been steadily increasing. How far does the increase in resources which this brings about result in increasing prosperity in all classes, irrespective of legislation and social arrangements? I.E. does poverty, and social inequality tend to correct themselves merely through the increased return which nature makes to human effort?

[1] Churchill deployed troops in urban areas affected by the 1911 strikes.

6 May. The difference between the standpoint of the upper
classes and of the working classes may be summed up as
follows: The former think they make laws because they were
the best educated, most leisured, most civilized class in the
community. The latter think the upper classes are civilized,
intelligent, and leisured, because they have the power to make
laws.

Modern politics are concerned with the manipulation of forces
and interest. Modern society is sick through the absence of a
moral ideal. To try to cure this by politics is like make [*sic*]
surgical experiment on a man who is dying of starvation or who
is poisoned by foul air.

Plan of a Book.

I. Cause of present unrest not simply economic, nor party-
political, but moral. This is shown (a) by attitude of
workers themselves (b) by attitude of sympathetic rich (c)
by tone of literature and philosophy (d) by examining our
own mind. The root of it is that (a) the external
arrangements of society appear to contradict what men
feel to be morally right (b) that they believe that these
external arrangements are not (like a bad harvest) the
action of natural causes, but due to human action and
capable of being altered. Just as individual suffers (Fox,
Bunyan) when his habits of conduct are in contradiction
to the conscience within him, so society suffers when its
objective institutions outrage the best ideals of the age.
The problem is to (a) deepen our individual sense of sin
(b) objectify our morality.

II. At what point does existing legal and economic order outrage our moral sense? Different answers (a) Poverty of large numbers of persons. But this answer unsatisfactory. Poverty not necessarily intolerable – and in fact much worse. (b) insecurity: this brings us nearer the mark; it introduces a moral and psychological element. But this does not account for sense of injustice; the peasant is insecure, but he curses the weather, not social institutions. (c) mere class jealousy. But this is least of all true.

III. The indictment brought by workers against modern industry is in essence that brought in all times against slavery: viz that under present arrangements men are used not as ends but as means.

27 May. I asked various people what was cause of social unrest. SAM SMITH[1] said 'It is largely a matter of example. It is the first step at which people hesitate. They have generally never been on strike before, and think it a much greater wrench than it is. When the first step is taken, other people follow by force of example.'

A NORTHUMBERLAND MINER: 'People have discovered that human society is flexible: they have got the idea of evolution; and they do not see why social institutions should not be adapted in accordance with their desires.'

3 June. The worthy Marshall remarks (*Economic Journal*

[1] Ruskin scholar, 1910–11; organizer and assistant secretary of Ruskin College in 1912.

1907[1] I think) to the effect that no elected body can do so
much in the way of stimulating economic progress as can a
strong-will[ed], enlightened, energetic, individual, who feels the
responsibility of business management resting undivided upon
his shoulders, and who can organize industry as he pleases.
Bacon and Strafford and Laud thought much the same. And
in a sense they were right. We paid for our rash interference
with the paternal monarchy by experiencing the politics of the
18th century. And in the same way, when we cut off the heads of
our industrial Lauds and Straffords, we shall probably for a
century or so have to put up with political jobbery and
ineptitude which at present is limited by the fact that large
spheres of national life lie outside politics altogether. But if one
is asked 'Was the Great Rebellion worth while?' there are few
decent Englishmen who would not say 'Yes'. And If I am
asked whether it is wise to depose the economic oligarchy which
rules most of us today at the risk of facing a generation of
disorder and inefficiency before the new régime has made its
traditions I answer 'Yes. This too is worthwhile.' All experience
seems to me to prove that people, or at any rate English people,
will not accept efficiency as a substitute for liberty.

---

[1] Alfred Marshall, 'The social possibilities of economic chivalry', *Economic
Journal*, XVII (March 1907), 7–29. Marshall wrote that 'no fairly good substitute has been found, or seems likely to be found, for the bracing fresh air
which a strong man with a chivalrous yearning for leadership draws into his
lungs when he sets out on a business experiment at his own risk' (p. 17).
Tawney was also undoubtedly offended by the following passage: 'But I am
convinced that so soon as collectivist control has spread so far as to
considerably narrow the field for free enterprise, the pressure of bureaucratic
methods would impair not only the springs of material wealth, but also many
of these higher qualities of human nature, the strengthening of which should
be the chief aim of social endeavour' (pp. 17–18).

10 June. The industrial problem is a moral problem, a problem
of learning as a community to reprobate certain courses of
conduct and to approve others.[1] This, it may be said, is
moonshine. But let us take a concrete example. Every one in
England today condemns slavery. Every one in England would
feel that a man who got his income from slaves, was doing
something disgraceful. Even when out of sight of civilization,
a man wld feel that to make money by trading in slaves or by
employing slave labour, was a thing he could not do and hold
up his head again. And this feeling against slavery, be it noted,
is quite independent of whether a man treats his slaves kindly
or not. However kind a slave owner might be – and he might
be much kinder than many English businesses – he is
condemned because he is outraging the deepest human
sentiment, the sentiment which forbids a human being to be
treated as a thing in law. Now one need not point out that
though this sentiment is very ancient, its appliction is quite
modern – in 1800 there were a great many people who saw no
wrong in slavery. Why should not the same sentiment grow up
towards the most characteristic immoralities of modern
industry? If an average decent Englishman feels that it is a
disgraceful thing to by and sell human beings to hold them
as his property, why should he not feel that it is a disgraceful
thing to exploit the labour of children, to take advantage of
unorganized labour to beat down wages, to take large profits

---

[1] Tawney taught a summer course at Leeds in June 1912 on 'Some strands of
modern political thought', which may have inspired these remarks. A year
earlier, he had given a similar course at Oxford; see Russell L. Jones, 'The
invasion of a university', *Highway*, III, no. 35 (August 1911), 173: 'Birkenhead,
Birmingham and Swindon, Belfast, London and Longton, are at the moment
grappling with R. H. Tawney upon the need for a unifying centre for ethical
precept.'

himself while his employers are housed like cattle? But it is not only the employer who is to blame. It is all of us. We see no wrong in taking dividends which are wrung out of the oppression of other people. Above all – and it all comes back to this – we see no wrong in using other people not as human *personalities*, but as *tools*, not as *ends* but as means. But this of course is the essence of slavery. Is it not possible therefore for us to widen our conception of slavery from legal rightlessness to practical helplessness, from property in human beings to property in the labour of human beings, and to feel the same moral abhorrence of the latter as we do of the former? This it seems to me is the fundamental question of the day. For what produces our social divisions is not mere poverty, but the consciousness of a moral wrong, an outrage on what is sacred in man. This is why thousands of men strike in order that justice may be done to a few, when they have everything to lose, and nothing to gain by striking.

One whole wing of social reformers has gone, it seems to me, altogether astray. They are preoccupied with relieving distress, patching up failures, reclaiming the broken down. All this is good and necessary. But it is not the social problem, and it is not the policy which would ever commend itself to the working classes. What they want is security and opportunity, not assistance in the exceptional misfortunes of life, but a fair chance of leading an independent, fairly prosperous life, if they are not exceptionally unfortunate. It is no use giving opiates or stimulants to men who [*sic*] daily regimen is unhealthy. It is no use devising relief schemes for a community where the normal relationships are felt to be unjust.

There is this difference between modern poverty and that of

earlier ages. In the 16th century a man might be – according to modern standards – poor; but he might, nonetheless be independent, in the sense of controlling the fundamental conditions of his own life. Today independence is an expensive luxury. To the mass of the people poverty means that the conditions of your work, and therefore of your life, are settled by someone else.

All decent people are at heart conservatives, in the sense of desiring to conserve the human associations, loyalties, affections, pious bonds between man and man which express a man's personality and become at once a sheltering nest for his spirit and a kind of watch-tower from which he may see visions of a more spacious and bountiful land. All decent people are against a creed which tries such things by the standard of 'utility' as though there were any end of life except life itself. What makes the working classes revolutionary is that modern economic conditions are constantly passing a steam roller over these immaterial graces and pieties, breaking up homes, casting venerable men on to the scrap heap because they are 'no good', using up children 'for their immediate commercial utility', and all in the name of material progress, that cotton may be cheap! They want the state to step in and put down these lawless vandals who judge human affection by their effect on the money-market. They want to 'conserve' the home, the property, the family of the worker. They do not belief [*sic*] that progress consists in 'changes which can be expressed in statistics'. No political creed will ever capture their hearts which begins by saying simply 'we will give you a little more money. We will still measure success by the old standards. But we will let you have more of it.' What is noble in the Labour movement is

.

precisely this, that when a man does sacrifice personal success – as many workmen do – to a cause, they do not think him a quixotic fool. They recognize that his creed is really their creed – and yet, how tragic is the cynicism which one often finds among them, cynicism expressed in the question 'What are you getting out of it?' They have seen human souls sacrificed so often to money that they have ceased to believe in any other motive except personal gain.

One of the things which strikes me as I grow older is the extraordinary truth and subtlety of the religious dogmas at which, as an undergraduate, I used to laugh. 'Original sin' that what goodness we have reached is a house built on piles driven into black slime and always slipping down into it unless we are building day and night. 'Grace' that wickedness in oneself is not overcome by willing: every day of one's life one learns this, and I at least forget it every day. Religious people say that one [*sic*] grace enables one to overcome sin. What seems to happen to one is this. As long as one is making an effort to overcome bad temper, one does not get on at all; at least I don't. Bad temper simply gets put on its metal [*sic*]. But if one relaxes the effort and so to speak, throws oneself flat and lets whatever power there is take possession of one and do with one what it likes, one's mind gets peaceful and smoothed out without a conscious effort. In fact 'grace' does what 'will' can't – all the discoveries worth making are as old as the hills.

The following story is authentic (I had it from Cartwright[1] 13 June 1912, who was told it by A. D. Lindsay,[2] in whose

[1] E. S. Cartwright, W.E.A. tutor in Oxford and secretary of the classes in the Stoke area.
[2] Then classical tutor and Jowett's lecturer in philosophy at Balliol.

presence the remark was made). Lindsay was consulting Strong[1] and Major ——, an official of Ch Ch,[2] re the accommodations in Ch Ch of students from the Tutorial classes. Major —— said 'I don't approve of it all. I don't know what things are coming to. I saw a letter addressed to my butler the other day, and it had Esqre after his name! I said to him, "John, what do you mean by receiving letters addressed Esqre? Kindly see that they are addressed properly in future."'

People seem to be as unscrupulous in economic matters in Oxford as they are elsewhere, underneath the varnish. Cartwright wanted a clerk for his office which is in Herbertson's[3] Geography school. A boy employed by Herbertson applied. He is 18, keeps a widow mother, and is paid by Herbertson 11/3 a week! Herbertson complains to Lindsay, to Cartwright, and threatens to complain to the V.Chancellor on the ground that Cartwright is tempting one of his employees to leave him, as though the lad were his slave, and had to ask his permission before trying to get more than 11/3!

But in urging the question whether we ought not to try some bold social experiments, it is not so much to the poor and bold spirits as to those who have leisure, have had opportunity to develop their faculties, have learned from history to realize that

[1] T. B. Strong, dean of Christ Church from 1901 to 1920 and chairman of the delegacy for the extension of teaching beyond the limits of Oxford University; instrumental in publication of *Oxford and Working-class Education* (1908). For Tawney's view on Oxford and the beginning of the W.E.A. cf. his series of articles, 'The university and the nation', signed 'Lambda', in the *Westminster Gazette*, 15–17, 23–4 February and 2–3, 10 March 1906 and his unsigned article in the *Morning Post*, 16 August 1907, 'Schools and scholars "Labour and culture"'. Mrs E. Morgan kindly drew our attention to these articles. [Eds.]

[2] Probably Major A. K. Slessor, then steward of Christ Church, Oxford.

[3] A. J. Herbertson, professor of geography in the University of Oxford.

there are golden moments in the life of mankind when national aims seem to be bent for some noble purpose, and men live at peace in the harmony which springs from the possession of a common moral ideal. I would ask them to think not of the misery of many today, but of the possibilities of joy and energy which every man knows to be in his fellow [*sic*] because he seeks them in himself. Let us reflect that all over the world there is a great struggle being waged between[1]

In the 17th century England upheld constitutional liberty when all other nations were passing under absolutism – 'England is the last country that hath a Parliament. Let it not perish now' – can we not teach the world the meaning of economic liberty in the 20th? We owe it to the world to try. For we led it into the moral labyrinth of capitalist industry.

22 June. The people who construct Utopias on the assumption that in the life of the future men will have so mastered nature as to [have] achieved undreamed of power and felicity err profoundly. They are worse than wrong. They are irrelevant. They do not only miss the mark. They fail even to see what the mark is which they miss. They do not only fail to find what they look for, but what they look for is not worth finding. The whole social philosophy which rests on the idea that the vital thing in the well-being of society is its material environment, and that power to modify that environment in an extraordinary degree is equivalent to power to live well is a doctrine which flies so plainly in the face of all human experience as hardly to deserve

[1] This paragraph is unfinished in the text; it is lightly crossed out but quite legible.

discussion. It is falsified by the whole course of economic history since 1750. During that period there has been a development of the power to control nature which, if it had been foretold in 1750, would have seemed not a whit less extravagant than the Utopias of today which tell us that we shall feed, clothe and house ourselves with 2 hours labour a day, that we [shall] turn the Sahara into an inland sea, and that we shall construct a new civilization in the air. But though I do not deny that the life of the mass of the people is richer and more varied than it was in 1750, I do deny emphatically that there is more contentment with it. I assert with some confidence that there has very rarely been a period when the existing social order was regarded with so much dissatisfaction by so many intelligent and respectable citizens as it is at the present day. And this growth of moral dissatisfaction has synchronized with an unprecedented growth in material resources. What is the conclusion? It is that what one may call a 'satisfying social system' is very largely independent of the material environment. The latter will not by itself bring the former, because the two things are not in *pari materia*. You cannot achieve a good society *merely* by adding one to one till you reach your millions. The social problem is a problem not of *quantities*, but of *proportions*, not of the *amount* of wealth, but of the *moral justice* of your social system.

This leads me to another point. If we cannot look for the realization of a peaceful and contented society merely in the diffusion of material well-being, where are we to look for it? I answer 'in rules of life which are approved as just by the conscience of mankind'. That is to say a poor society may be a very happy and contented society. A rich society may be a very

unhappy and discontented society, because the springs of
happiness and contentment are to be found not in the power of
man to satisfy wants, but in the power of man to regard his
position in society and that of his fellows with moral approval or
satisfaction. England in the middle ages was poor, incredibly
poor, poor with the poverty of an Irish peasant. It saw
starvation close. No rain in April and May, and it will be upon
us in September and October. But it was (I believe) fairly happy
and contented. Why? Because the social order was not revolting
to the consciences of most contemporaries. Now my complaint
of most modern prophets, Utopists, sociologists is this, that
they never tell us *why* we regard the present social order with
disapproval, or *how* we may produce a social order in which the
human conscience may find satisfaction. They tell us the causes
of poverty and how to cure it. They do not offer us any
certainty that when we have cured poverty we shall be better
pleased with ourselves.

30 June. The greatest mistake we make with our lives is to
snatch at the particular objects we desire. We grasp this that or
the other for fear that the opportunity of obtaining it should not
recur and we should be without it for ever. But the mere fact
that in the possession of such and such a thing our happiness
seems to be involved, shows in itself the absence of the inner
peace without which happiness is impossible. We are too
anxious to choose the direction in which our destinies shall
move, and we underrate the greatness of our own nature in
supposing that if thwarted here, or foiled there, it will not find
its own channels of expansion. If we realized the riches that lie
within every one of us we should know that we can all afford to

be spendthrifts of nine-tenths of the possessions which we treasure, success, praise and good opinion among men, achievements, and still more material well-being. By the mere law of its own nature and development every human character is every day entering on a new world of treasures. But our appreciation of them depends on our ability to keep our hands of [*sic*] snatching at them, and too often in our haste to grasp the few pearls that we see we destroy the light which is needed in order to show the riches of which they are but the scattered 'inconsiderable items'. One cannot enjoy till one ceases to desire, for desire clouds the soul, and though we seem to ourselves to have achieved satisfaction in obtaining what we want, we have too often merely closed one of [the] windows through which the vision of a wider world was borne upon us. We are like men who deliberately shut out the light in order that it may not show that the diamonds which they wear are made of paste. This sounds melancholy. Really it is optimism. It means this 'Never be afraid of throwing away what you have. If you *can* throw it away, it is not really yours. If it is really yours you cannot throw it away. And you may be certain that if you throw it [a]way, whatever in you is greater than you will produce something in its place. Never be afraid of pruning your branches. Trust the future and take risks. In moral, as in economic affairs, the rash man is "he who does not speculate".'

9 July. An engine-driver from London: 'I was active last summer in the Railway Strike. When we went in, we were promised the same jobs before [*sic*] or not worse ones. Directly I got back, I was sent for, and was taken off my number 4 engine (the highest grade, an express) and put on to number 3, and the

management has since then been training non-unionists to take the place of other men. I lose 12/- to 18/- a week by the change. But it is a question of "management", and the Conciliation Board are not allowed to deal with questions of management, but only with hours and wages. We can appeal to Sir Guy Granet[1] through the Board of Trade. He will no doubt be fair about it. But all the officials are against us.'

10 June [July].[2] A COMPOSITOR FROM LIVERPOOL: 'I will give you two examples from my own experience of the way in which unemployment is produced. I have been through 2 crises. The first was the introduction of the linotype. The company (a newspaper) for which I worked put in 11 machines and cleared out about 30(?) men. Some of them got regular work elsewhere: several of them dropped into being casual workers. I met one the other day. He had been doing jobbing work at newspaper offices ever since. The second crisis arose from the amalgamation of the *Herald* with the —— (another paper). Before the amalgamation the *Herald* was a very good office to work in: men made £3 a week, and were their own masters. When amalgamation took place about 100(?) men were sacked straight away. The shareholders made a very good thing out of it. The paper has been paying good dividends ever since. Many of the men were ruined and became casual workers. Some of the older men went home and died in 6 months. Various reasons were given by the doctors. But I know the cause. It was "amalgamation". That is going on all over the country and in

---

[1] General manager, Midland Railway Co., from 1906; helped set up the Railway Conciliation Scheme of 1907, the breakdown of which was the immediate cause of the 1911 railway strike.

[2] June is almost certainly a slip of the pen for July.

every trade. Wealth is being concentrated: productive power increased, and the people is [*sic*] becoming poorer.'

People often talk as though the effect of trade unionism or of legislation protecting the workers were to produce a weaker, less enterprising, type of employer. This however is by no means necessarily the case. In the completely unorganized trades what happens is that the employing classes develope [*sic*] an extraordinarily overbearing, tyrannous, and irresponsible habit of mind, which is extremely bad for themselves and productive of a most anti-social arbitrariness and self-will. They will make their own terms with labour; and when they have done this for some years they will make their own terms with the community. Then managers and servants catch their attitude. They climb into favour by harshness and bullying and by repressing every symptom of independence, every attempt at organization among the wage-earners. Workmen are regarded as 'servants', and when they strike they are said to be 'disloyal', to be 'rebelling', to be 'treacherous'. Now this attitude is really a public menace. It lowers the whole tone of national morality. It encourages the idea that the mass of the people are 'productive' tools. It makes the wives and even the children of the upper classes overbearing and inconsiderate and lawless. One of the first lessons we need to impress on the rich is that they have got to be *disciplined* into being servants of the public. We must recover the idea of the position of the landlord and employer being a *post*, an *office*.

21 July. The fundamental idea of Liberty is Power. Power to control the condition of one's own life. Whether this [is] thought of as the removal of restrictions imposed by the state and minor

sanction (individualism) or as the imposition of restrictions (collectivism) is a matter depending on the economic and political circumstances of periods and classes of people. It took men 150 years and two revolutions to arrive at some working conception of religious liberty. It may take us as long to work out our idea of economic liberty.

July. Drew, of Castleford [*sic*], a colliery engineman, took an active part in the coal dispute, and was sacked. He applied for work in another colliery. A clerk in the office, a friend of his, showed him a letter from the firm where he had worked, asking that he should not be employed by any firm in the district.

26 July. A COMPOSITOR FROM LONDON: 'I know a man who made an invention by which two lines of type, large and small could be set by the same matrix. The linotype is the property of a single firm which has combined with firms in America and Germany. He had no option but to dispose of the invention to them. They gave him a few pounds for it. Now the firm charges £50 to every business on whose linotype machines they fix it.'

28 July. MOORIES[1] told the following tale to illustrate the futility of the minimum wage act. 'Two brothers I know worked in a "place" at a colliery. The place was abnormal; largely dirt. One week they made no wages. They applied to the firm, and they were made up in accordance with the act. The next week they applied again: the firm refused to pay and simply said "If you don't like the place, there are plenty of others who will take it." For 3 weeks they worked without any wages.'

[1] Probably J. B. Moories, a student in Tawney's Stoke tutorial class.

31 July to 1 August. MRS WEBB: 'What is the root idea of socialism? The ideal of my parents, good intelligent people, was that we should get on. They honestly thought that this was not only best for oneself, but best for the world. I should say the essence of socialism was the substitution of the ideal of service for that of getting on.'

S. WEBB, in answer to questions whether he expected a labour majority: 'No, and I am not sure it would be desirable. After all there must be a division of labour, even in government. A certain number of labour members are [*sic*] very useful. But it does not follow that the House should be predominantly composed of them.'

IDEM 'It may not be possible to raise wages very much. But there is no reason why the community, by public provision, should not make the life of the ordinary workman as rich and interesting as that of the fellow of an Oxford college: put the heritage of all the ages in his hands.'

IDEM 'We always say that if only one gets rid of the 3 or 4 millions at the bottom, the social problem wld be almost solved.'

12 August. The proper way in which to approach the social question is to ask how is it that so many good men come to quite different conclusions as to the nature of our present social order and as to their duty towards it. The desire to order [?their] life rightly exists in most men. How is it that every day good men are doing what seems to equally good men wicked? It may be said that this has always been so, and that these differences are but the differences of political opinion which by their very

diversity make up a richer unity. Unfortunately however this is not the case. It is quite true that there must always be diverse groups and parties in a nation, that different traditions, mental aptitudes and experiences will result in different political doctrines, and that the existence of such variety, by offering a wide field of opinion from which to select, is the best guarantee of national wisdom. But while it is inevitable, and indeed desirable, that men should differ as to means, it is not a welcome thing that they should differ as to ends. Variety in political opinion is beneficial. Variety in standards as to fundamental questions of conduct is not, for it does not only divide parties, but poisons social life, and causes one man to earn his bread with a bitter sense of injustice, while another stops his ears to the grievances of his neighbour. Unity, in short is to be desired in all those matters which involve the everyday life of mankind, not in the sense that all must believe the same things or act in the same way, but in the sense that one man must not suppose that what another believes is dictated solely by selfish interests. While disapproving of his actions he may be able to see that it has a moral justification. It is just this moral justification which is lacking to the economic life of today. It is just the lack of it which turns disagreement into discord and·bitterness.

27 August. Our governors should remember the words of Bacon[1] 'The blessing of Judah and Issacher will never meet, that the same people or nation should be both the lion's whelp and the ass between burdens.'

[1] From *Bacon's Essays* (ed. J. M. McNeill, 1959), p. 85, in 'Of the True Greatness of Kingdom and Estates', Also used by Tawney at the end of his article 'Prussianism in the schools', in the *Daily News*, 14 February 1918, reprinted as 'Keep the workers' children in their place' in *The Radical Tradition* (ed. Rita Hinden, 1964).

4 September. When one considers the need for finding some
moral standard in economic life, one is inclined to think that
perhaps the world ought to return to the idea of voluntary
poverty and renunciation; that it ought to suspect wealth;
ought to idealize the self-abnegation of those who are satisfied
with little; that a nation like England should, in fact, voluntarily
lower its standards of living to contentment with harder, more
meagre, fare; in short that we should escape from the moral and
economic evils of capitalist industry by ceasing to be a great
industrial community and living the life of Switzerland or
Denmark. I mention this idea only to discard it. It cannot be the
will of God that we should lay down the powers and resources
which we have amassed, or that we should deliberately break
up, as such a lowering of economic potentialities would break
up, the empire. We cannot recover from our economic position
merely by surrendering it.

What alternative remains?

The case for the existing industrial system is the case for
autocratic government all the world over. It is efficient: it saves
trouble: responsibility is placed in few hands: there is no
nonsense about consulting committees. Marshall's words (*Ec Jl*
1907)[1] as to the effect of complete irresponsibility on an able
man put exactly the case as it must have presented itself to
Strafford who would have had Charles govern 'free and
absolved from all rules of law'.

9 September. W.H.B.:[2] 'The well-to-do represent on the whole

[1] See above, p11., n. 1.
[2] W. H. Beveridge, Tawney's brother-in-law, author of *Unemployment. A
Problem of Industry* (1909) and then an official of the Board of Trade,
reponsible for labour exchanges. Later Lord Beveridge.

a higher level of character and ability than the working classes, because in the course of time the better stocks have tended to come to the top. A good stock is not permanently kept down: it forces its way up in the course of generations of social change, and so the upper classes are on the whole the better classes.'

How does this view correspond with the actual facts of social history? Take the land system. The 'better stocks' presumably became masters at the Norman Conquest, while 'the worse stocks' became (very largely) serfs. In what sense are the words 'better' and 'worse' used? In the 15th century the peasantry grew in prosperity: in the 16th century they declined, and in places were almost swept out of existence to make room for large estates. The reason given for this by the economic historian is fairly simple. It is that a new and very profitable method of using land paid the upper classes (landlords and merchants) better than the traditional system of agriculture, and that being almost omnipotent in admini- stration they could have their way, with the result that the bulk of the peasantry were impoverished. But one cannot assert that the upper classes were able to make parks, enclose for pasture and thus build up great fortunes because they were the 'better stock', or that the peasants, who up to 1450 had been prosperous, became after 1450 the 'worse stock'. Again from 1688 to 1832 England was governed (in domestic matters) mainly in the interests of the landed gentry; from 1832 onwards mainly in the interests of the commercial classes, and the opportunities which individuals possessed of rising were largely determined by the system of government obtaining. It is surely difficult to argue that the triumph of the landed aristocracy in 1688, and of the middle classes in 1832 were in each case a triumph of the 'better stock', and that the possibility of a 'better stock' coming to the top of society in 1760 (say) was in no sense dependent on the fact that political power was concentrated in the hands of a particular class.

Further the 'better stock' presumably moves upward through its own efforts. It comes to the top (as I understand the argument) by merit. But is not political agitation to be included in those efforts, and has [*sic*] poverty and adverse economic and social conditions, themselves the result largely of political power, no effect in repressing merit?

Finally at what date are we to conceive the development of society to such a state that the better stock comes to the front to have been completed? Those who hold this theory usually talk as though at the present moment the upper classes consisted of the better stocks. But have the upper classes *always* consisted of the better stocks? (If so the present governing classes, who are different from those who governed 200 years ago, would appear to be necessarily worse merely because they are different.) If not, when did this happy state of society, in which the better stocks inevitably come to the top, become established?

(It will be observed that throughout I am arguing on the assumption that the phrase 'better stocks' is free from ambiguity.)

If the 'stock' is the only thing which matters, how does a 'stock' which flourishes in one set of economic conditions, become degraded in another (e.g. the handloom weavers, the landholding peasants)?

16 September. The following books want writing:

(i) An account of the agrarian revolts of 1549. Russell's book[1] is goodish. But there must be a lot of material in the record office bearing on Somerset's agrarian policy, which he didn't use.

(ii) The social politics of the Commonwealth period, with special reference to the Levellers and Diggers. Gooch knows the authorities,[2] but nothing (it appears) about the economic conditions. I suspect one could trace both movements straight back to the earlier agrarian changes. I must look up Bernstein's book.[3]

(iii) The rise and development of the idea of 'Laissez-faire' and the movement away from the state policy of the 16th century. I wonder if Puritanism produced any special attitude toward economic matters. I believe Schulze-Gaevernitz has some remarks on this.[4]

(iv) The economic policy of the period of personal government 1629–1640.

(v) The intellectual antecedents of 19th century liberalism – in economic matters (see iii).

---

[1] F. W. Russell, *Kett's Rebellion in Norfolk* (1859).

[2] G. P. Gooch, *The History of Democratic Ideas in the Seventeenth Century* (Cambridge, 1898).

[3] Eduard Bernstein, *Kommunistiche und demokratisch-sozialistische Strömungen während der englischen Revolution des 17. Jahrhunderts* (Stuttgart, 1895).

[4] G. Von Schulze-Gaevernitz, *Britischer Imperialismus und englischer Freihandel zu Beginn des zwanzigsten Jahrhunderts* (Leipzig, 1906). For a later statement of his views, cf. his *Democracy and Religion* (1930), p. 15: 'In matters economic Calvinism opened up the way for the capitalist revolution. Thus Calvin – and the fact is significant of the economic changes of his epoch – abandoned the prohibition of interest on loans by his explanation that in many instances a loan is more profitable for the debtor than for the creditor. So Calvin and his followers in New England became in effect protagonists in the cause of Capitalism, and paved the way for the cleavage between the classes and even slavery.' Max Weber is not mentioned in any of Tawney's pre-war writing.

18 September. I am inclined to think that a great deal of thought and discussion which goes by the name of sociology has very little value so far as the improvement of human life is concerned, not because it is untrue, not because the problems with which it deals are unimportant, but because information – of a more or less speculative character, about the probable consequences and tendencies of human arrangements is, by itself, not very likely to make those arrangements better. What is needed for the improvement of society is not so much that men should have profound information as to the possible result of their actions, but that they should have a keen sense of right and wrong, that they should realize that the conceptions 'right and wrong' apply to *all* relations of life, including those where their application is most inconvenient, such as those of business, and that they should act on their knowledge. More knowledge [?we'll] certainly need. But what we need still more is the disposition to act on the knowledge which we possess; and I am disposed to complain with regard to sociologists generally that they concentrate attention on remote consequences instead of on immediate duties, that they substitute inexpediency for sin and social welfare for con-science, and that then the world instead of feeling that it is a miserable sinner, flying from the city of Destruction, escapes its responsibilities today by speculating on the probabilities of the future. Now I do not complain of all this intellectual activity being applied to tracing out social actions and reactions. What I do want to drive home is that our conduct in particular cases is, and must always be, very largely independent of it, and that therefore the first step towards an improvement in social life is to judge our social conduct by strict moral

standards. I venture to say – though it sounds a heresy – that
there [are] certain sorts of behaviour which we know to be
right, and certain others which we know to be wrong. Let us
act on what we know. We know it to be wrong for a man to live
as though the effects of his actions upon his neighbours did
not concern him. We know it to be wrong for one man to
deceive another in order that thereby he may obtain pecuniary
advantage. We know it to be wrong for one man to take
advantage of the weakness of another in order to wring out of
him terms to which he would not submit if he were a free agent.
This knowledge is, I would urge, the common property of
Christian nations. If it is asked, on what it is based, I answer
that it is based on the experience of life in all the principal
nations of Western Europe, and that its validity is shown by
the fact that when these propositions are stated in a general
form, nobody in practice would venture to deny them. Not
only so, nobody, in practice, would think it necessary to appeal
to the consequences of neglecting them in order to prove their
validity, though it is I suppose, on the consequences of
neglecting them that their validity ultimately rests. Very well
then – what is the task of the sociologist? It is [I] submit to
show how these universally accepted principles may be
applied to particular sets of social conditions. It is in fact
analogous to the business of a jurist. A jurist builds up the
body of laws, by bringing new cases, as they arise, under some
of the general principles of his science. A sociologist ought to
build up his science by bringing new economic cases under
some of the rules of conduct generally accepted by civilized
men. This does not appear to me to be done at the present
time. What is happening is that there is great activity in

investigation both inductive and deductive (– to use bad
words –). But that the new facts are largely useless so far as
conduct is concerned, because they are not grouped under the
established principles by [which] most men admit that their
conduct should be controlled. Let me take one or two examples:
What were the reasons for the abolition of slavery? (I have no
special knowledge on this point and must look it up) They
were, I suppose, that a body of opinion which [*sic*] arose
which held that the employment of one man by another as a
tool was immoral, and that this body of opinion became
sufficiently powerful to convert the majority of persons, who
had never realized that slavery implied this, and those who, if
they realized it, had never made in their minds the connection
between this fact and any accepted principle of morality, in
such a way as to reveal to them that the fact and the principle
were inconsistent. The reason for the abolition of slavery was
certainly not that after calculation the advocates of the change
arrived at the conclusion that its abolition was more profitable
than its maintenance. They acted as they did because they
believed slavery to be *wrong*, and believing it to be wrong
determined to get rid of it irrespective of whether the result
would diminish or increased [*sic*] – it actually increased – the
productive capacity of the slave or the profits of the quondam
slave-owner. Now let us turn from this example to another.
Everyone at the present day knows a large number of persons
are paid wages which makes it extremely difficult to live
virtuous lives. They are tempted to neglect their duties to their
families because it's so hopeless to discharge them, or to be
mean for fear of neglecting them, or to be quite casual because
they will not be mean, according to their temperament. In

practice the vices of slave labour tend to appear among them. They feel they are treated unjustly: they have no prospects; and the employer tries to make up for the absence of other incentives by close supervision. We are, in fact, as I am inclined to say, faced with a problem analogous to, though different from, that which confronted the Abolitionists.

How far is it possible for us to approach it in the same spirit?

21 September. A man asks his labourer to hand him bricks. 'Pass up those bricks, Bill, will you.' The Boss, passing, 'Not so much of your bloody "will you".' (Told Clay by Thomson of Halifax)[1]

6 October. The peculiar characteristic of the wage system, which marks it off from earlier methods of production, is that everything which is in the nature of a surplus over the lowest price at which his labour can be got tends to be abstracted from him. When most men were small landholders or small craftsmen, this was not so. They took risks. But at the same time they took profits and surpluses. At the present day the workman takes risks, the risk of unemployment. But he has not got the prospects of exceptional gains, the opportunities for small speculation, the power to direct his own life, which makes the bearing of risks worth while. It is a recollection of this fact which supplies the answer to those who say that in protecting the worker against the risks of industrial life, the state is undermining his independence. It is quite true that the bearing of risks is bracing, *if it is voluntarily undertaken,*

[1] Henry Clay, then W.E.A. tutor in industrial history at Rochdale and Leeds. Thomson of Halifax has not been identified.

because in that case a man balance[s] probable gains and losses and stakes his brains and character on success. But when the majority of persons are hired servants, *they* do not decide what risks they shall bear. It is decided for them by their masters. They gain nothing if the enterprise succeeds: they have neither the responsibility of effort nor the pride of achievement; they merely have the sufferings of failure. No wonder that, as long as this is so, they desire above all things security, and since they have no opportunities for enterprise and reap none of its profits, desire chiefly to be guarded against its dangers. In such circumstances the plea that men should be allowed to take risks because it braces their character and calls for the fine qualities – which is true – is an attack not upon modern attempts at giving the wage-earner greater security, but upon the whole wage system, which exposes him to losses without offering him profits, which gives him all the disadvantages of insecurity without the compensatory advantages of the opportunity of self-direction.

The supreme evil of modern industrial society is not poverty. It is the absence of liberty, i.e. of the opportunity for self-direction: and for controlling the material conditions of a man's life. This produces poverty, because it produces hopelessness, irresponsibility, recklessness. That is the lesson of the industrial revolution and of the enclosures. To give men the *will* not to be poor, we must first of all give them the control of the material conditions on which their lives depend, that is set them free.

What I want to drive home is this, that the man who employs, governs, to the extent of the number of men employed. He has jurisdiction over them. He occupies what is really a public office. He has power, not of pit and gallows, and infantheof [infangthief] and outfantheof [outfangthief], but of overtime and short time, full bellies and empty bellies, health and sickness. The question *who* has this power, how is he qualified to use [it], how does the state control his liberties, how far it makes the kings' writ run inside his franchise, this is the question which really matters to the plain man today. And this power is at present possessed and exercised quite at haphazard. Anyone may wield it who can command sufficient capital. We insist on our civil servants having certain qualifications. Diplomatists must have good manners and understand French. But there is no provision that our employers shall understand the language of the people they govern, and as for manners!

One might elaborate this subject in the following ways: Call it 'the Nature of freedom in an industrial society'.

I.   Industrial serfdom.

II.   Serfdom and poverty (the psychological causes of poverty).

III. The revolt of the serf.

IV.   Industrial freedom. The question of the *government* of industry is much more closely connected with the question of poverty than is usually supposed.

V.   The ethics of the question: the moral attitude produced in society by the present system.

14 October. There was a time (if we may trust fairy tales) when poverty meant freedom. Today poverty means slavery. That is why reformers glorified poverty in the middle ages, and why they denounce it today.

Economists sometimes tell us that the market value of an article, being the expression of its marginal utility, represents the urgency of the want which is felt for it, and seem to imply that production, if guided by prices, will produce those articles which are most urgently needed. Price, in this theory, is the link between needs and resources: it determines how the latter shall be used to satisfy the former.

Now it is, of course, perfectly true that prices do express the urgency of the consumers' demand. But it expresses only the demand of those consumers who can pay, and expresses it in proportion to their ability to pay. A high price does not mean that a thing is desired by many people. It may (and usually does) mean that it is intensely desired by a few. The effect on the market is exactly the same in each case. And this reveals rather a profound chasm between our moral standards and the exigencies of economic practice. Our moral standards require that each man should count for one and no more than one; that one man's demand should be as good, as 'effective' as another's; that the resources of the community should be used to satisfy all, and not earmarked for the satisfaction of a few. In economic life however the demand for goods of one man does not count as one. It counts as nothing, or one hundred, or according to the degree of his wealth. What is clear is at least this. 'That an article fetches a high price is no indication that it satisfies an urgent social need. It may merely be satisfying the whim of a millionaire. Hence value itself *depends* on the distribution of wealth, and if a rich man says "I became rich by supplying wants and my riches are a proof of the degree of my service", we must answer by asking "service to whom?" You cannot justify the inequality of income merely by arguing that large incomes are the payment for meeting urgent wants, because one may answer that many of these "urgent wants" are urgent only because wealth is already so unequally distributed.'

People often meet demands for the abolition of some social evil by saying 'things even out. Wages may be temporarily depressed, but in the long run they will rise. Trade fluctuations produce unemployment, but the dislocation is only temporary. In the long run it corrects itself.' Of all imbecile attitudes this is the most imbecile. A similar argument would show that there was no need to punish robbery, because everyone has a chance of becoming a robber, and because in the long run people will ensure against the risks. What we ought to feel about unemployment or low wages is what decent people feel now, when there has been a gross miscarriage of justice. We ought to feel that no subsequent compensations can atone for the outrage to humanity as represented by the individual who is the victim.

16 October. The view of the causes of poverty to which I am coming is that they are to be sought in the existence of economic privileges which give those who enjoy them a lien or bond on the labour of those who do not. Just as in mediaeval society the foundation of the aristocracy was the revenue drawn by: 1. from [sic] the villages on which it was imposed, partly from political power (curial revenue) partly by economic monopoly (profits of mills, fisheries, etc.) partly by the mere relation of lord to serf (chevage, merchet and the rest); so in modern society the principal cause of the inequality of wealth consists in property rights which enable those who enjoy them

to impose a toll on those who do not. The principal foundations of economic privilege are

    (i)   the right to receive the product of superior sites.

    (ii)   the right to direct industry, without reference to the convenience of those engaged in its executive processes, and with a regard solely to the interests of those who have property in it.

    (iii) the right to bequeath and accept bequests.

This list does not, of course, pretend to be exhaustive or to be a scientific classification. But it is I think that obvious that all the three points mentioned have the effect of conferring a right to wealth produced by others without any corresponding return *necessarily* being made. Before, however, condemning this state of things, one must know that it has been and is qualified by two facts. (a) The classes enjoying economic privilege do to some extent render, and have in the past rendered, a return for them. That return has been, as it were, a matter of grace. They have continued to enjoy their privileges even when it ceased to be made. But the fact that it has been made is of course [of] enormous importance, and in considering how far these privileges are worth maintaining, one has to take account of it. Thus, in the past the great feudatory rendered valuable service: the country gentleman was the backbone of 16th and 17th century administration; the ducal landlord who administers his estate stands today in a very different position from the urban landlord who is a mere rentier; the entrepreneur of the early 19th century, savage and predatory animal though he often was, had the same use that a cunning and energetic bully has in a mining camp. He kept a sort of order and got the work done. (b) The effects of economic privilege are often mitigated by public opinion and by the law, which leaves their foundations intact, but intervenes to prevent their results being too intolerable. The great disadvantage of such intervention is that it is usually capricious, arbitrary, onesided, based on the relative power of different sections of the unprivileged orders to force attention to their claims, or on the chance sympathies of the privileged classes, rather than in any thought out attempt to remove the evils which most cry for removal. Still it has had a powerful effect in mitigating extreme abuses of power. In earlier ages the monopolist has been controlled by the intervention of the state to fix prices, and the money lender by its prohibition or restriction of usury. In our own day the factory acts are a similar example.

Taking, to start with, the position indicated above, what are the obvious lines of reform? They are surely, first of all, to remove the economic privileges through which some classes get rich at the expense of the public. This seems to me to involve (a) an inquiry into the methods by which public can be substituted for private ownership of land, at least in those cases where private ownership is divorced from actual administration; (b) an inquiry into the economic effects of the transmission of inherited wealth, and the extent to which it is and can be mitigated by taxation; (c) an inquiry into the effects of the existing monopoly of higher education; (d) an inquiry into profits in certain selected industries, with a view to discovering how many firms are making profits above the competitive minimum and what they amount to.

When one has dealt with the results of economic privilege, *then* is the time to go on to investigate questions connected with the facts of poverty, as they exist today. One would start

(a) by setting out *why* modern poverty is specially detestable (mediaeval poverty: the poverty of fishermen or crofters today – often is not).

A large part of modern society is engaged in the gentle pastime of buying gold too dear, and another part in that of selling other people's blood too cheaply. The result is riches.

A motto for Directors of all kinds.

> 'All ignorant they turned an easy wheel,
> Which set sharp racks at work to pinch and peel.'[1]

A great many poor people are 'inefficient'. This means that they do not correspond to a standard of efficiency erected by their masters, the rich. Why the devil should they?

22 October: It was once said in my hearing 'After all, squalid as the industrial struggle is, it is redeemed by the fact that a man carries it on not only for himself, but for his wife and children, for a group, the family'. Truly a sapient defence! Most murders, forgeries and robberies have been made with the same unselfish purpose.

The merits or demerits of an industrial system are not to be measured solely, or even principally by the success with which wealth is distributed among the parties involved in it, but by the extent to which the relation existing between [them] are such as to develope [*sic*] self-respect, self-reliance, mutual

---

[1] The same phrase is used, in relation to the vices of sub-contractors in the chain-making industry, in Tawney's pre-war study of that trade: *The Establishment of Minimum Rates in the Chain-making Industry under the Trade Boards Act of 1909* (1914), p. 62.

confidence and enterprize. It is true that the presence or absence of these relations and qualities will depend to a great extent upon the degree to which individuals receive a share in distribution adequate to satisfy their material needs. But when this has been granted, the fact remains that certain economic relations are in themselves preferable to others, irrespective of the wealth which they confer. Nor is it an adequate remedy for a faulty economic relationship merely to increase the share of wealth received by the poorer or worse paid of the two parties. The reason why such a remedy is unsatisfactory is this. The method by which one's income is obtained is as important as the amount of the income itself. Every decent person recognizes this in their own life, when they have a choice. One can buy gold too dear. If the way one earns one's living involves a complete loss of liberty, the living is not worth earning. Now in modern society a great many people are buying gold too dear every day of their lives – or rather something which passes as gold – and this fact embitters them. That is why so many working people idealize the age before the rise of the great industry. It is not mere ignorance. It is that they are dimly aware that *no* income – much less theirs – is worth a life which one regards as unjust from top to bottom. It is not merely the toil they resent, but the dependence and subservience.

23 October. People justify themselves for throwing up causes by saying that they must consider their children. But what of their children? When they grow up must they consider theirs and sneak cautiously through life for the same reason? Must the world never be improved by anything more than the small contributions which each generation makes before it marries?

Is it one's duty to one's children to leave the world as bad as one found it?

26 October. The secret of growth is self-surrender, and as much so in matters of intellect as in matters of morals. If a man wants to do serious scientific work in any sphere, he must become impersonal, suppress his own fancies and predilections, and try and listen to reason speaking in him. But whatever the cause, religion, science, faith in social progress, the elevation of a man out of himself into a world where there is no rivalry but only service, is the supreme human good.

There are two elements in economic freedom: (i) control of conditions under which you will live, (ii) choice of the conditions, etc. Up to 1642 or so emphasis was laid on (i). In the 19th century it was laid on (ii).

30 October. What may a modern community expect from its Universities?[1] It may expect [?three] things. First, that it should uphold exact and arduous standards of knowledge. Second, that it should make those standards operative in the world at large by teaching. Third, that it should so organize itself as to make intellect and character the sole passport to its advantages. To put the matter in another way, the business of a University is two-fold; to uphold an *intellectual* standard, and uphold a *moral* standard. The intellectual standard it upholds by maintaining a severe intellectual discipline. The

[1] Tawney's interest in university reform may be traced in the materials which Dame Henrietta Barnett sent to him for the chapter in the *Life* of her husband, cited above (p. 7, n. 3). The documents are among the Tawney Papers in the British Library of Political and Economic Science, London School of Economics.

moral standard it upholds by making that discipline accessible
to all who will submit to it, by relaxing it for none merely
because they are well to do or socially influential, by depriving
none of it merely because they are poor or uncouth or socially
incompetent. In this way a University might become a centre
of moral authority. And it is precisely such moral authority
which Englishmen need more than anything else at the present
time. We require to (a) be taught the infinite difference
between what is false and what is true; (b) think of knowledge,
like religion, as transcending all difference of class and wealth;
and that in the eye of learning, as in the eye of God, all men
are equal, because all are infinitely small. To sell education for
money is the next thing to selling the gifts of God for money.

3 November. Every community should have a body of bridge-
builders, pontifices, a very good name, for the bridge-builder
is the real priest. These are the beavers of society, unobtrusive
gentle animals, yet with sharp teeth and bright eyes, eyes to see
where piles must be driven, what stout timber must be felled.
Where the bars to bind and fasten must be set, teeth to cut
down obstructions and bite them into place. It is said that the
devil builds bridges, and I certainly think that social bridges
are not built by men without any devil in them. But he is a
good labourer devil, a lubber fiend who does more work than
most of the Saints in the Calendar. Never were a gang of
bridge-builders needed more than now!

This is the supreme paradox of religion that it sets men
changing the world for the better who believe that from eternity
to eternity all is well, that it sets in the forefront of revolutions

those who believe that one great revolution has freed men once and for ever, that it makes faith into a crusade, and [sets] spurs to men who [are] winning the holy city because they know that in every city however unholy there is God. Great achievements proceed not from the mind that merely aspires, but from the mind that it [*sic*] is at rest. They are the fruit not of hope or fear, but of confidence. Their motto is not 'I will', but 'I must!'[1]

10 November. The 'Distributive State' consisting of small property holders, master craftsmen and peasants, is a very attractive ideal. Belloc[2] is quite right in saying that in the middle ages what the public conscience desired was not efficiency of production, but a wide diffusion of property. But it had two great drawbacks. In the first place, in a society composed largely of small property holders, the man without any property, the wage-worker, usually leads a dog's life. This was so in mediaeval England: witness the Statutes of Labourers, the assessments of wages, the restriction on mobility, the compulsion to labour (which Belloc denounces as characteristic of the Servile State). These forms of oppression were popular with the town bourgeoisie and the country yeomen. It is so in Ireland today. The 'Patsy Farrells' are at the mercy of the small landholder, as much as the English labourer is at

---

[1] cf. the following passage in *Religion and the Rise of Capitalism* (1926), p. 109:
'The central paradox of religious ethics – that only those are nerved with the courage needed to turn the world upside down, who are convinced that already, in a higher sense, it is disposed for the best by a Power of which they are the humble instruments – finds in it [Calvinism] a special exemplification.'
[2] Hilaire Belloc, *The Servile State* (1912). Belloc was associated with the literary journal *The New Age* to which he and his fellow Roman Catholic, G. K. Chesterton, contributed scathing critiques of collectivist socialism.

the mercy of the great farmer and landlord. The 'distributive state' is good for the property holders. But they are a privileged class who probably (if one may judge by the past) would tyrannize over the classes who have no property. Further it does not favour equality. For it leaves the bases of inequality, economic rent, in the hands of private individuals.

2 December. The stages of thought about social affairs through which I, and I suppose other people, have passed are something as follows. One begins by regarding poverty etc. as a matter of individual misfortune. One does not connect it with the main institutions of society; nor does one think of those institutions as the work of the state and dependent upon its support. One therefore does not look to the state for improvement. In the second stage one realizes that then there is a unity underlying the individual cases of poverty; that they are connected with social institutions, specimens of a type, pieces of a system, and that this system is, in the first instance, the work of the state and can be altered by an alteration of the law. One therefore now looks to the state for reform. Just as the first stage was that of the C.O.S.,[1] so this is the stage of the theoretical socialist. In the third stage one realizes that the attitude of the state is just the attitude of countless individuals, that to rage against it for not removing economic evils (which state action can remove) is as futile as it is to rage against the Pope for not being a reformer, and that society cannot lift itself up by the soles of its boots. The attitude of governments to social questions is wrong, profoundly wrong. But it is wrong because the attitude

[1] The Charity Organisation Society, which Tawney contemplated joining in 1903 after he went down from Balliol.

of individuals to each other is wrong, because we in our present
society are living on certain false and universal assumptions;
and that even when statesmen honestly mean to do [?good]
they will often do harm (apart from bad luck, miscalculations
etc.) merely because all their actions, good and bad, proceed
from a character based on those assumptions. What we have
got to do *first* of all is to change those assumptions or principles.
This is where I think the Fabians are inclined to go wrong.
They seem to think that you can trick statesmen into a good
course of action, without changing their principles, and that by
taking sufficient thought society can add several cubits to its
stature. It can't, as long as it lives on the same spiritual diet.
No amount of cleverness will get figs off thistles. What I want
to do is to get clear in my mind what those moral assumptions
or principles are, and then to put others in their place. They
are

(i)   That a man is not responsible for the results of a course
of action pursued in the course of business; provided
such action is compatible with the law, that he cannot
be blamed for it: the denial of responsibility.

(ii)   That a man may legitimately be employed to realize an
end which he would not pursue, except under the
pressure of fear of starvation, and that the mass of
mankind are property treated as 'hand', or rather,
now, as tools: the denial of personality. (It will be
observed that (i) and (ii) are really converse propositions. If a man *is* a tool, he cannot be held or hold
himself responsible.)

(iii)   That there is no standard of justice, equity, or fairness
in economic transactions but that the fact that a

transaction is made is the justification of its being made: the denial of other than individual morality.

(iv) That as long as men are well-fed and housed the nature of the social relations which they enter in order to earn food and housing does not matter: the denial of freedom.

We in England ought to sympathize with the world-wide movement of Labour, because it is aiming at the very objects which we used to boast that we had attained. We look back with pride, or we used once to look back with pride, at our dealings with the Stuarts. We forget the dogmatism of Pym, the brutality of Cromwell, the intolerance of nearly all of that great time, because behind it all we see that men were striving for freedom, for the right of men to live their own lives and express their own personalities which is what freedom means. The labour movement, behind all its froth and its intolerance, really stands more than any other movement, for freedom today. What it demands is that men should not live their lives at the will of a master. The way in which it seeks to attain it is the old English way of the rule of law, that there shall be a settled constitution, that thousands shall not be dependent on the caprices of a few, like slaves, but that they shall have a voice in settling the conditions under which they may live. This is what the appeal to the State, the Socialism which frightens so many good souls, really means. 'The question in dispute between us...was whether...the nation be governed by force like beasts; or whether the people should be governed by laws made by themselves, and live under a government derived from their own consent.' He who employs governs, and has a jurisdiction measured by the number of people he employs. Our claim is that he should not 'Govern us by force like beasts', but that 'the people should be governed by laws made by themselves'.

13 December. The demand for a minimum wage marks the extraordinary barbarism of our economic arrangements. It means that people are not to be paid what they are worth, but what is necessary to keep them working. That is how a horse or a slave is paid.

1913

5 January. ALLINGHAM:[1] 'Sympathy is a priceless commercial asset. The firm which does not show sympathy with its workers will not get the best out of them. The firm which does will.' Therefore the self-interest of employers will act as a guarantee that they will be 'sympathetic'!

G. UNWIN:[2] 'Liberty means opportunity to make the world different. Everybody ought to have a chance of this. But it can only be done with much pain and anguish. Many are called but few are chosen. To me it is incredible that committees and elected persons can ever manage the higher life of mankind.'

R.H.T.: 'On the other hand they can put down tyranny. We need a power to reduce to order the great industrial feudatories.'

G.U.: 'Yes. But, I am afraid lest the old criticisms about the levelling tendencies of democracy may prove true. The South African war gave me an awful impression of the possibility of whole peoples moving to destruction. I dislike very much all

[1] Not identified, possibly a chain manufacturer.
[2] George Unwin, professor of economic history at the University of Manchester since 1910.

attempts at social reform which treat mankind in the lump or mass. I do not want the sentimentalities of life to be over-ridden. Progress seems to me to depend on the new middle classes not demanding swiftly more material wealth. They can't have it, and that way lies revolution. Certainly there has been an enormous improvement since the '70s in housing, dress, and amusements. But I fear very much such things as the state regulation of higher education.'

6 January. Here is an elementary problem which baffles me: In what [?way] *ought* the fruits of economic progress to be distributed between worker, employer, and consumer? The view of the employer is that he ought to buy labour at the lowest market price. He is genuinely scandalized at the idea of (say) paying turners 38/– to do work which a machineman can quite well do at 26/–. The view of the worker, on the other hand is 'Why should the employer get the advantage of labour saving machinery rather than the employee? It is all very well to say that ultimately it will be transferred to the consumer by a reduction in prices. But the employer will prevent it from being transferred as long as he can.' Of course these are common-places. But the difficulty is a real one. Suppose one were a public body in a similar situation. What wld one do?

Expressed in the most general way my subject is 'the relation of the efficiency of labour to the conditions under which it works'. This involves (a) an account of the history – min^m wages – shorter hours, etc. (b) a study of the contemporary conditions, (c) an investigation into methods of costing – which I might get from Allingham or Renolds.[1]

[1] Renolds Ltd, Manchester chain manufacturers.

7 January. It ought to be possible to place certain principles of social and economic conduct outside the sphere of party politics, as matters agreed upon by the conscience of the nation. In certain departments of public affairs, we do this already: e.g. the maintenance of a navy, and to a less extent, general foreign politics. Could not one find some formula expressing the attitude of all good men to social questions, which should be so entrenched in public conviction as to be drawn into dispute by no party?

6 February. A great many social reformers are occupied in casting out devils with the aid of Beelzebub, by explaining that justice (in moderate amounts) really pays, and that what is wrong with the world is not that it is too much guided by selfishness, but that its selfishness is not sufficiently enlightened. That it *does* pay I believe is true. Yet to put the matter in this way is to sell the things of God for gold. Happily or unhappily there is usually no purchaser. For strange though it seems, it is nevertheless a fact, that in 99 cases out of 100 the man who is guided by self-interest is incapable of receiving the enlightenment which alone would show him where his true self-interest, even on the narrow commercial plane lies. A man must be a little mad even in order to act with common sense. A man must be a little altruistic even in order to appreciate the full possibilities of selfishness. To the employer who is concerned only with his own gain the possibility that his work people will work better if they trust and respect him more is unintelligible. It is not until he has felt the hunger for justice in himself that he is capable of understanding that others will respond to his just treatment of them. That is where the mere economics of social

50

reform – Fabianism etc – the whole 'science of means' breaks downs. They tidy the room, but they open no windows in the soul.

? February. KEELING:[1] 'You say that the only thing worth doing is to secure a rise in wages. I don't agree. Look at the miners. Their wages have risen very largely. But their social life is much less satisfactory than that of workers who earn less, e.g. textile workers' (he was thinking primarily of the woollen industry).

25 February. A book ought to be written on some such subject as this: the economic foundations of aristocracy; the causes of economic inequality; the foundations of economic privilege. What I want to know is: (a) what makes the difference between countries like Denmark where there is substantial equality, and countries [?like] England and America where there is not. What are the institutions which make the difference (if it *is* institutions)? (b) the effect of certain great experiments in removing inequality, e.g. the abolition of feudal rights in France. Acton says it added 60 per cent to the average income of the peasants.[2] Did it?

26 February. Mr R. H. Glassfield (4–6 Brick Lane E)[3] made

[1] Frederic Hillardson Keeling, author of *Child Labour in the United Kingdom* (1914), and assistant editor of the *New Statesman*. Killed in action during the First World War. See also *Keeling Letters, and Recollections* (1918) edited by his mother-in-law, Emily Townshend.

[2] Lord Acton, *Lectures on the French Revolution* (1910), p. 100: 'The France of history vanished on August 4, and the France of the new democracy took its place. The transfer of property from the upper class to the lower was considerable. The peasants' income increased by about 60 per cent.' In November 1913, Tawney began to teach a course on the French Revolution to his Longton tutorial class. The syllabus and lectures of this course may be found among the Tawney Papers.

[3] Not identified.

some interesting remarks revealing the successful businessman's philosophy. 'As Rudyard Kipling says, it is the law of the jungle, the survival of the fittest. Strength comes to the top.' He quoted Herbert Spencer. He seems to take a sort of satisfaction in regarding competition in business as reducible to a philosophy.

The line which intellectual socialism has hitherto followed in England has been collectivist, not communist. It has concentrated on state regulation – the policy of the national minimum. It has almost surrendered the policy of communal ownership and use, except with regard to certain local services which offer, when in private hands, special opportunities of fleecing the consumer. Now this policy increases the well-being of the classes who are protected, and I have no positive objection to it. But it does not touch the problem of inequality based on economic privilege which is, I think, even more than poverty, the great blot on modern society. I do not see how that can be attacked except by a large transference of property rights, by the adoption of the principle that economic 'rent' is not to be left in private hands, and that there shall be sufficient equality of opportunity to prevent the maintenance of 'plum' posts where payments are high because entrants are artificially made and kept scarce. What I mean is (a) the municipalization of urban land and the regular purchase of land by the state (b) the purchase of coal-mines and railways and licensed houses (c) the creation of a really democratic system of higher education (d) heavy taxes on incomes from property. What I don't see is any sign of a force making for these changes. They are certainly what the working classes mean by socialism. But then 9/10 of them have not got to the point of realizing that our present (though not all) inequalities are the creation of man not of God. The middle class reformer is either (a) moved by pity of the poor and merely anxious to relieve their sufferings (b) interested in 'tidying up' regulations, organization etc (c) convinced that principles are valueless and only a fool looks more than 12 months ahead. The fact is that what we want is a restatement of principles.

27 February. England is the country in which the middle classes triumphed earliest and became established most securely. The result of this has been that in some ways England has most leeway to make up in dealing with questions of economics and property. In Germany a parliamentary government (of a kind) based on a wide franchise followed hard on the heels of absolute monarchy, and mediaeval municipal institutions. Hence the property of the former was never distributed and remains for the nation. In England the property of the Crown and of the monasteries was at a fairly early date distributed among the middle classes. Hence we have not merely got to keep it for the nation: we have got to recover it.

6 March. An aristocracy is proud. A pseudo-aristocracy is vain. The English upper classes are vain.

In order to believe in human equality it is necessary to believe in God. It is only when one contemplates the infinitely great that human differences appear so infinitely small as to be negligeable [*sic*]. To put it in [an]other way, the striking thing about man is that he is only a *little* lower than the angels themselves. When one realizes this it is absurd to emphasize the fact that one man is, even so, lower than another. One can't look a gift cherub in the mouth. What is wrong with the modern world is that having ceased to believe in the greatness of God, and therefore the infinite smallness (or greatness – the same thing!) of *man*, it has to invent or emphasize distinctions between *men*. It does not say 'I have said, "Ye are gods"!' Nor does it say 'all flesh is grass'. It can neither rise to the heights or descend to the depths (these meet in a spiritual exaltation which may be called either optimism or pessimism). What it does say is that *some* men are gods, and that some flesh is grass, and that the former should live on the latter (combined with paté de fois gras and champagne), and this is false. For what elevates or depresses, what makes man regarded from one point of view seem an angel and from another an ape, is not something peculiar to individuals, but characteristic of the species, something which cannot distinguish between men, precisely because it is inherent in man.

People say that a belief in human equality means anarchy. In reality it is the one foundation of human subordination, of order, authority and justice, and it might more reasonably be attacked by those who love license than by those who fear [?for] liberty. For a belief in equality means that because men are men they are bound to acknowledge that man has claims upon man, that nothing can justify my using power which chance gives me (the chance of a majority as well as of wealth or birth) to the full, that nothing can justify my using my neighbour as a tool, or treating him as something negligeable [*sic*] which may be swept aside to realize *my* ends, however noble those ends may be. It means that of all revolutionary schemes there is one awful criterion: 'It were better that a millstone were hung about your neck and that you were cast into the sea than that you should offend one of these little ones'; that I may not *force* any man to do right, because, even though he [be] rich and wicked, he is still a man; that I may not compel any man, however foolish, to think as the wise think, because truth has been hidden from the wise and revealed unto babes. It means that not wealth or power or numbers or learning is the standard by which conduct must be judged, but the conviction of the individual conscience; and that mercy, humility, peace, love shall judge cleverness and strength and numbers.

To put it more prosaically. Order involves the recognition of obligations. But obligations are only recognized where there [is] identity of nature. I have no duties to a tiger* or to a fish*. This identity is what I mean by equality. *Compulsion* which seems to be the basis of order, is not really its basis. Where there is *mere* compulsion in human society, as in parts of the modern industrial world, there is not order but disorder, ending, in extreme cases, in what we call revolutions. Where there is order compulsion is only the outward generalization of the individual's sense of right. A rule of the road is compulsory; but no one except a fool wants to break it.

(*This is 'without prejudice' to dogs and cats, which need a separate treatise)

13 March. Justice pays – if one is just enough (S.A.B.)[1]

26 March. A.L.S.[2] said 'people complained of the corruption, immorality, inefficiency of the clergy for 500 years before the

[1] S. A. Barnett. See above, p. 7, n. 3.
[2] A. L. Smith, Jowett fellow and tutor in modern history at Balliol, whose opinions on medieval history were shared by Tawney.

Reformation. The Reformation did not come *till the citadel was attacked.*' This saying seems to me profound, and true of most revolutions. Too much time is spent today upon outworks, by writers who pile up statistics and facts, but never get to the heart of the problem. That heart is not economic. It is a question of *moral relationships*. This is the citadel which must be attacked – the immoral philosophy which underlies much of modern industry.

21 April. One illustration of 'the heart' which must be attacked I heard today from Hookway[1] and Clay. At Denaby main there are two pits. At those 2 pits no union labour is employed. The company owns a large number of houses (v. the case of evicting miners). It owns the public houses and pays the manager a commission on the amount consumed. I am not sure if it owns the advowson: but any way the parson says that his work would become impossible if he had a disagreement with the manager. If this is not a 'public jurisdiction in private hands' what is? Yet there are 8 labour members on the local authority. How tiny is their power compared with the despotism conferred by the ownership of property! And how long will people be content for the appearance and the reality of power to remain separate?

People want rights – freedom, in order that they may perform duties. The hardship of the wage-earner is not simply that he has insufficient food and housing, but that he is deprived of the means of performing certain primary duties, care of home, wife

---

[1] E. J. Hookway, assistant secretary of the W.E.A., shared Tawney's flat in Manchester.

and family, direction of the industry by which he lives, a share in public life. Hence the way of freedom is also the way of duty.

One knows from one's own inner experience, that spiritual well-being consists in finding one's work and doing it. This involves subordination, and therefore subordination is of the essence of a good society. What we all want is freedom to serve; for 'God and the king have not given us the poor living we have, but to do service[s] therefore among our neighbours abroad'.[1] In this idea, 'freedom to serve', rights and duties are reconciled.

5 May. A[2] is like a halfpenny paper, three parts advertisement and the rest sensations and misrepresentation. The only difference is that he cries himself and doesn't bother about a halfpenny provided he can find a public.

Whiggism in domestic politics was simply feudalism using constitutional means.

6 July. If anyone says 'the working classes are better off than they were 50 years ago, why should they agitate? What material is there for a revolution?' I answer that all experience shows that the probability of a revolution is not proportionate to material grievances of the country in which it takes place. A revolution occurs when there is a violent contradiction between the external political order, and men's subjective

---

[1] From *A Discourse of the Commonwealth of this Realm of England*, ed. E. Lamond (Cambridge, 1893), p. 14. One of Tawney's favourite quotes, also cited in *Religion and the Rise of Capitalism*, pp. 169–70.

[2] Possibly the Prime Minister, Asquith, who was said to have broken down and wept during the final stages of the Commons' debate on the settlement of the miners' strike in 1912. See George Dangerfield, *The Strange Death of Liberal England* (2nd ed., 1966), p. 238.

conception of right. It is due therefore as much to a change or development in the latter, as to a deterioration in the former. This is the spiritual factor in human development, which our own economic age tends to forget, and forgetfulness of which is ruin. It is ruin for this reason; that it leads men to suppose that changes *within* the existing order, which improve material conditions, are a substitute for the change *of* the order itself which is felt or thought to be immoral. In proof of the first point, that revolutions are not timed or proportioned to material grievances, one might quote (a) the American Revolution: the colonists had far smaller grievances than the inhabitants of almost any European country; certainly far smaller than the vast majority of Englishmen from 1793 to about 1823. They rebelled because the English colonial theory was inconsistent with what they had been in the habit of considering their rights, and because from 1760 onwards this theory was forced upon them by administrative and legislative changes. (b) The French Revolution. It is a commonplace to say that the French peasantry in 1789 were better off than many German peasants and than they themselves had been earlier in the century. The revolution had behind it, it is true, vast economic and material grievances, horrible wickedness, cruelty, and mis-government. Nevertheless it was in essence the uprising of a new system of ideas, was based on new standards, without which material injustices would not have been revealed as so intolerable, and was dominated by a new conception of human possibilities.

In proof of the second point I offer the suggestion that governments are usually least oppressive, and most considerate just before their fall. They are dimly conscious that a new and critical [?spirit] is abroad and they endeavour to save the order with which they are identified by removing the most obvious grievances and encouraged enlightened administration. In this they are usually aided by the 'cultivated' classes, the humanitarians whose feelings are more easily stirred by hardships than their consciences are by injustice, the experts who hope to push their plans but will do [so] most easily if there is no general *bouleversement*, the moderate men generally. The physiocrats and Turgot are the type I mean in France. In England there was something of the same kind of thing in Bacon and Strafford.

Such changes within the existing order are never, however, accepted as a substitute for the overthrow of that order, once it has generally come to be regarded as unjust, i.e. as inconsistent with certain fundamental human claims, (which are prior to government in logical order, though posterior to them in time). The reason is that, at bottom, Western peoples will not accept material progress as an alternative to and substitute for, freedom. The two things are, in fact, incommensurable, necessaries of a different order, and to offer the former instead of the latter is simply irrelevant. In fact it usually intensifies the demand for the latter by suggesting that the government itself has qualms, is ill at ease, and conscious of its weakness. This fact is realized now in relation to certain groups of problems: e.g. colonial government; where self-government is now (though not till after 1776) taken as a starting point; and political arrangements: no [one] now suggests (except as regards women) that consideration for the needs of the governed is a substitute for political freedom.

It is not however realized that the same standards must be

applied to economic arrangements. In this matter people still talk as though a rise in wages compensated people for dependence upon the will of a master whom they cannot control. In fact, however, it is just the power to control the material and spiritual conditions of one's own life, which is meant by freedom, and as long as this is withheld no amount of material progress will reconcile people to its absence.

22 July. As long as individuals think the attainment of moderate material comfort the chief end of life, so long will governments plead as an excuse for not doing this or that that they cannot afford it. If modern England and America are right in believing that the principal aim of man, what should be taught to children, what should serve as a rough standard of merit, what merits approbation and respect, is the attainment of a moderate – or even immoderate – standard of comfort, and that moral questions arise only after this has been attained; then they must be content to go without religion, literature, art, and (I wld add) learning. These are not hard to find for those who really seek them, or who seek them first. But if they are sought second they are never found at all.

Of course these are all commonplaces. What I mean is that the failure of society to make the changes which are obviously important when regarded in bulk is due to the fact that individually we all have a false philosophy of life. We assume that the greatest misfortune which can befall a man is poverty – and that conduct which leads to the sacrifice of income is unwise, impractical, etc; in short that a man's life should be judged by its yield of income, and a nation's life by its production of wealth. Hence we have had one group of economists who have attacked certain reforms on the ground that they diminished wealth, and another school who answered them not by saying 'let wealth be diminished, fiat justitia', but by arguing that they really would not diminish wealth after all. The answer is I believe correct. But it is, nevertheless, devilish; for it suggests that human life, justice, etc. should be measured as items on a balance sheet.

It will be said: 'abolish economic privileges, and there will be enough wealth for all to live, and for all to lead a spiritual life.' This, I take it, is the Webbs' view. Now economic privileges must be abolished, not, primarily, because they hinder the production of wealth, but because they produce wickedness. But supposing unearned incomes, rents, etc. are pooled, will not the world, with its present philosophy, do anything but gobble them up and look up with an impatient grunt for more? That is the real question. It will not be faced in my lifetime because as long as the working classes believe, and believe rightly, that their mentors rob them, so long will they look on the restoration of the booty as *the* great reform, and will impatiently waive aside more fundamental issues, as a traveller robbed by a highwayman declines to be comforted by being told that money, after all, does not buy happiness. But when their masters are off their backs they will still have to face the fact that you must choose between less and more wealth and less and more civilization. Sometimes they have to face it now. Cotton operatives have to decide whether shorter hours are worth a reduction in wages; cooperative societies whether they will spend their divi on education.

Again may not it be that the real way to overcome the power of the wealthy is to despise wealth?

When three or four hundred years hence mankind looks back on the absurd preoccupation of our age with economic issues with the same wonder as, and juster contempt than, we look back on the theological discussions of the middle ages, the names which they will reverence will be those of men who stood out against the prevalent fallacy that the most important problems were economic problems, and who taught men to conquer poverty by despising riches.

29 July. Since men exercise their activities on a planet the space of which is limited, and since they live by working up resources the supply of which is limited, it is inevitable that their material interests should frequently collide; because one man desires that which is desired also by another. The fundamental question of political ethics is, then, is there any standard by reference to which the desirability of subordinating A to B, or B to A, may be decided, or to put it otherwise, what is the principle [?which][1] the party against whom the decision goes is bound to recognize. In practice, however, since individuals are too easily bound by custom, too unoriginal, or too timid, to question the justice of the principle applied to the particular cases in which they immediately are concerned, and since it is only groups, parties, and movements of men which put forward alternative principles, the question more normally appears as 'what is the standard by which the relative merits of different arrangements of human affairs are to be judged?' When we talk of distribution being bad, of wages being unfair, of exploitation, of sweating, what in fact do we mean?

To this ancient question nearly the whole of the modern

[1] Text reads 'to'. Presumably 'that' or 'which' intended.

world appears to give the answer 'the greatest happiness of the greatest number' including those who dislike Bentham and those who have never heard of him. As far as the English socialists, in particular, are concerned, they have taken the criterion of public well-being straight from Bentham almost without question, and their criticism of the radical individualists has taken place within the limits of this formula, and they have contented themselves with arguing, in my opinion successfully, that to attain the *end* proposed by Bentham, or to satisfy the Benthamite *criterion* of well-being, other means than those proposed by Bentham must in fact be followed. Thus they have turned the weapons of the individualists against themselves, and have tried to show that while the standard by which human arrangements must be judged is their contribution to the well-being of the majority – interpreted mainly in material terms, that well-being is more likely than not to be attained by increased action on the part of the state. They have, as it were, said 'True that economic system which promotes the well-being of the majority most is best. Only you do not really understand the methods to be used. When you are as clever as us, you will not change your ends: you will adopt our means.'

Now I do not propose to discuss what is meant by 'greatest happiness', or to draw subtle distinctions between happiness and pleasure. Nor am I concerned to deny that the Benthamite formula is a good working rule, a good first approximation, a convenient parallel to open against fortresses of privilege. But it appears to be defective in several ways, and its defects seem to be to produce, in view of its general acceptance, grave practical consequences.

First. Are all institutions which are for the greatest happiness of the greatest number *ipso facto* good? Suppose slavery carried out by a large race of conquerors over a small minority benefited the former, wld this justify it? Suppose cheap goods could only be obtained by tolerating brutalizing conditions among those who produce them, are those conditions justified? Suppose the wealth of a white nation is increased by the ruthless exploitation of a small backward race, is that exploitation justified? To these questions I answer 'no', and I think most people would agree with me. But I do not see how such an answer can be reconciled with Bentham's principle. Now any one section of oppressed workers is in relation to the whole community a minority. Bentham's rule seems to me to supply a justification for continuing to oppress them eternally.

Second. The principle has an appearance of simplicity and decisiveness, which is, in fact quite illusory...

Third. As long as one remains in the sphere of interests no reconciliation of conflicting claims is possible...

The acceptance of the principle appears to me to arise from a confusion between the *method* by which what is judged right is ascertained, and of the *standard* by reference to which a thing is judged right or wrong.

If it be asked what is your criterion: why do you condemn this and approve that? I answer that the standard which we apply is really a transcendental, religious, or mystical one. When we condemn slavery, sweating, the exploitation of a weak race by a conqueror, *even though these things are convenient* to the greatest number concerned, we do so because we recognize that the convenience of the majority, and the destruction of the life of the minority are really incommensurable, and that *no* amount of convenience to the former can justify *any* injustice to the latter. Why is this? Because the personality of man is the most divine thing we know, and that to encroach upon it is to efface the very tittle [*sic*] deeds of humanity. This is the principle we do recognize in part, and which we ought to recognize everywhere and always. There is a law higher than the well-being of the majority, and that law is the supreme value of every human personality as such. This is what is meant by saying 'it were better that a millstone should be hanged about your neck and that ye shld be cast into the sea than that ye shld offend one of these little ones'.

This conclusion leads to some practical results.

(a) It diverts attention from 'happiness', which is vague, to right and wrong which are clear. It is a modern fad to suppose that before you can act you must know all the consequences of your action. To hesitate to prevent say slavery, or sweating, for fear that you may do more harm than good, is like stopping to consider whether, when a robbery or murder is taking place, it is not really better for the victim to suffer, because he may be a bad man. The rule is clear '*no* convenience can justify *any* oppression'. Act on this. If you stop to consider whether in other ages and places some unseen consequences of your act may not harm someone you will never act at all. The whole of our industrial life is tainted with the vice 'do evil that good may come' (or rather on the chance that good may come). E.g. people justify the oppression of individuals by arguing that it means cheap production. Even some socialists reply by arguing that it does not *really* mean cheap production, and then admit the premise that if it meant cheap production it wld be justified. But [it] is this premise which is wrong. One may *not* do evil that good shld come. It is *not* expedient that one man shld die for the people. If business is conducted, as it is, on the principles of Macchiavelli [*sic*], that self-preservation justifies all wickedness, the only right course is to discard the principle, not, as some socialists do, to dispute its application in particular cases.

(b) Once it is admitted that economic conduct is simply one branch of conduct, and the reform of economic evils becomes a matter in which every individual has a part, a duty, and a responsibility, we are all either doing right or doing wrong. Which we are doing each of [us] has to decide in accordance with his conscience. He may be mistaken in his application of his standard, but he is not tempted to deny that there is a standard, or that he is amenable to it. And this is a great gain, for mistakes are corrected by experience, but the denial of the existence of a standard is an error in fundamentals, in direction. The farther he proceeds, the more astray must he go. If, on the other hand, a man is asked to judge his conduct by whether it promotes the 'greatest happiness of the greatest number' he is asked to do something impossible and so does nothing at all. He leaves it to politicians, who are supposed to [be] specialists in the art of discovering what makes the greatest number happy. And this in fact stultifies politicians. For a good law is a rule which makes binding objectively conduct which most individuals already recognize to be binding subjectively. And when individuals do not recognize any standard by which economic conduct is to be judged, any moral issue at all, the material out of which good laws can be made is non-existent. The unreality of modern politics – by which I mean their failure to appeal to noble and important emotions and beliefs –

is due to the fact that men have tacitly denied for about a
century and a half that any moral issue is raised by the
relationships and branches of conduct with which politics are
largely concerned. Politicians cannot rescue men from the
vacuum which a false philosophy has created, for men cannot
lift themselves by holding the soles of their boots.

10 August. T.W.P.[1] said 'there is danger in the materialism
of the socialist movement. It will not be seen in this generation.
But since this generation has thrown off doctrinal restraints
(i.e. formulated beliefs of religion) the next generation may go
on to deny the spiritual basis of life altogether.'

  'Moral conduct by itself is not enough. Unless a man
believes in spiritual things – in God – altruism is absurd. What
is the sense of it? Why shld a man recognize any obligation to
his neighbour, unless he believes that he has been put in the
world for a special purpose and has a special work to perform
in it? A man's relations to his neighbour become meaningless
unless there is some higher power above them both.'

13 August. The essence of all morality is this: to believe that
every human being is of infinite importance, and therefore
that no consideration of expediency can justify the oppression
of one by another. But to believe this it is necessary to believe
in God. To estimate men simply by their place in a social order
is to sanction the sacrifice of man to that order. It is only when
we realize that each individual soul is related to a power above
other men, that we are able to regard each as an end in itself.

[1] T. W. Price, Midland secretary of the W.E.A. and lecturer at Birmingham
  University.

In other words the idea of 'humanity' stultifies itself. The social order is judged and condemned by a power transcending it.

20 August. W.T.:[1] 'To love another person means to desire that they shld be themselves.'

As a nation's industrial system is, so will its philanthropy be. Industry creates poverty by refusing to treat men as ends or respect their personalities. And when charitable people start relieving the poverty which an individual system of industry has produced, they show as great a contempt for the rights of personality as do the organizers of industry themselves. They seem to be alleviating distress while they really are the embodiment of the principles by which distress is produced.

27 August. The detailed research into social conditions on which the modern world spends so much labour throws a small beam of light on the road immediately before us. The direction in which we are moving is determined by quite other moral and intellectual causes whose springs lie deeper. We ought to turn these for strengthening and refreshment more often than we do. It is probable that the constitution-making of 1789 would have been more judicious if it had been preceded by a more serious inductive study of political science; if Sieyès, for example, had not thought that he had said the last word on that subject. But the loss to the world had there been no appeal to fundamental philosophical ideas wld have been incalculable.

[1] William Temple, then president of the W.E.A. and headmaster of Repton School from 1910; Tawney's contemporary at Rugby and Balliol and future archbishop of Canterbury.

10 September. Marxian socialists are not revolutionary enough. They say that capitalist society is condemned because the worker does not get the equivalent of what he produces. He does not. But why should he? The real condemnation of the capitalist spirit is contained in the suggestion that men should get only what they produced. As though we were shareholders in a goldmine to be paid according to our holdings of stock! A barbarous, inhuman, sordid doctrine that wld weigh immortal souls and scale them down because they are not economically useful. God forbid that they shld be! This doctrine means that wealth should go to those who care for nothing *but* wealth, and are therefore least fit to have it.

15 September. When the first settlers imported slaves to America, they thought 'here is a chance for dividends.' The result has been centuries of misery, a civil war, burnings and lynchings, and perhaps another and more terrible war before this century ends. We see this now clearly enough and say that it is righteousness which exalteth a nation. Do we realize that 200 or 300 years hence historians will point to the 19th century capitalist as we point to the first slavers?[1]

7 November. I see that Pringle in the *Economic Review*[2] uses the figures supplied by the Census of Production as an argument against agitation to redistribute wealth; on the ground that it shows that as a nation we are really poor, and that the

---

[1] Tawney began to teach 'The secession of the American colonies' to his Longton tutorial class in late 1913. These lectures may also be found among the Tawney Papers.
[2] Rev. J. C. Pringle 'The census of production and Labour propaganda', *Economic Review*, XXIII (October 1912), 393–401.

primary need is to increase wealth. This may be an answer to a certain school of social reformers. But it is not an answer to me. For (a) the poorer we are the *more* the need of securing equality. On a desert island or in a shipwrecked boat men must be put on rations (in the middle ages they were virtually put on rations. That was [what] the regulation of food supplies, the assize of bread etc. meant). (b) The problem of modern society is a problem of proportions, not of quantities; of justice, not of material well-being. Peace comes not when everyone has £3 a week, but when everyone recognizes that the material, objective, external arrangements of society are based on principles which they feel to correspond with their subjective ideas of justice.

3 December. The most pressing problem of our day, and the most neglected, is that of economic right, not of economic facts. But during the last half century nearly all English thinkers have devoted their whole attention to the collection of facts, not to the examination of the nature of economic right. It is time that the current were change[d]. There is no alchemy by which force can be transmuted into right, and in our calculation of forces we have forgotten that the human mind demands not explanation only but justification of all established orders and all schemes of progress. That is to say, the question of our day is a philosophical rather than an economic one.

People often argue that the industrial system is justified by its 'efficiency'. But this [is] the shallowest of claptrap. For what is at issue is not whether it is efficient, but whether it is just. If industry could be so organized that the mass of workers would feel convinced that the social order was just, a decrease in efficiency wld be cheap at the price.

11 December. Man's spiritual nature needs an outward organization as well as his material one. Therefore there must be a Church as well as a State. But the church must not be above the state, not because it is too bad but because it is too good, not because it is too weak, but because it is too strong, not for the sake of the state, but for the sake of itself. Its position is defined in the words 'He that is greatest among you let him be the servant of all.' The church cannot help being powerful: but it can help trusting the arm of the flesh. It must be free to be a servant. The ancient question whether church is to be above state or state is to be above church, finds its solution in a free church refusing the temporalities for the sake of the spiritualities.

I see Wells[1] is writing in some magazine a paper on what the world will be when science has trebled our wealth. It is astonishing how people can go on believing in the face of all the evidence that society can be appeased by filling its stomach, by adding one to one. It never has been and never will be, because the social problem is one of proportion not of magnitudes. Conversely I am not much perturbed by the question what will happen to Great Britain when she has exhausted her coal, or when other countries consume their foodstuffs and raw materials at home. We shall be poorer, of course. But if we have pursued justice we shall be happier. While if we have not, we shall be no happier than we are now, however rich we are.

[1] H. G. Wells, 'The world set free', *English Review*, XVI (December 1913), 13–42.

To my question whether he thought we had in his experience advanced towards any solution of social problems (an awful phrase), whether things had in his experience got noticeably better, Graham Wallas[1] answered 'the improvement was more rapid between 1840 and 1880 than it has been since. Recently real wages have fallen. But I do not see why there should not be so much equality in England as, I understand, obtains in Norway. It is not fair to confine one's attention to wages. The London child is given an education costing £5 per head. That means that if a parent has 4 children, he is really given £20 on account of them. Again the budget of 1909 was really a very bold step. The Americans were quite alarmed by it.' (But the London workman did not *want* to be given £5 for the education of each child. Besides, it is not £5 net, for one must deduct the wages which the child would have earned.)

There is no such thing as a science of economics, nor ever will be. It is just cant, and Marshall's talk as to the need for social problems to be studied by 'the same order of mind which tests the stability of a battleship in bad weather'[2] is twaddle.

1914

8 January. The problem is to find some principle of justice upon which human association for the production of wealth

---

[1] Professor of political science at the London School of Economics; one of the original Fabian essayists and founders of the Fabian Society.

[2] Alfred Marshall, *The New Cambridge Curriculum in Economics and Associated Branches of Political Science: Its Purpose and Plan* (1903), pp. 12–13. In a discussion of the effects of keeping wages artificially high through restrictive practices and other means, Marshall noted: 'What is needed, and what we may hope is coming in the near future, is a larger study of the same kind and by the same order of minds as are applied to judging a new design for a battleship with reference to her stability in bad weather.'

can be founded. In the past there have been two main doctrines: (i) that which rested it upon prescription (traceable, ultimately, to be force), which assigned economic privileges to different classes, and which was swept away by the French Revolution; (ii) that which rested it upon individual choice and consent, which resented all intervention as an infringement of individual right, and which naturally led to the view that every form of association is justified if individuals enter it without legal compulsion and if no party holds economic priviliges peculiar to himself. It is this doctrine which is now on its trail. Its weaknesses are obvious. (a) It take[s] 'consent' as its justification, as against prescription. But it does not inquire under what conditions consent is a reality. In fact the mass of mankind are still driven, as ever, by hunger and fear. (b) It does not carry through its attack on prescription to the logical end. For while it is quite true that the terms of economic association are now normally settled by agreement, the economic resources of the parties to the agreement are usually so disparate as, in effect, to prevent its being free. But, it will be said, granted that this is true, yet there is at least equality of opportunity. Under the old régime not everyone could legally become a noble. Under the new régime everyone can legally become a landlord and a capitalist. This answer is, however, superficial. In the first place, as a matter of history, nobility was purchasable before 1789 in France, and this fact did not mitigate, but rather aggravated, the attack on privilege. In the second place the existence of social privilege is nonetheless irksome merely because the members of the privileged class vary from time to time, and because they sometimes include persons who have been drawn from the unprivileged classes.

To put the case more clearly: by privilege I mean payment, whether in money or social position, without corresponding services, and producing *pro tanto* economic power over the lives of others. This necessarily exists in any social system where property is highly concentrated, and it is perpetuated by the law of inheritance in England. The result of it is that the economic conditions of the unprivileged classes are determined not by consent, but by *force majeure*. This, it may be said, has always been so, because man has always been at the mercy of nature. The answer is valid as a retort to those who direct their attack primarily against *poverty*. It is not sound as against my argument. For in modern society the individual is not face to face with nature. Between him and nature stands a human superior. And though the amount to be shared depends in the main on 'nature', the terms on which it is shared depends upon human institutions.

What is necessary in order that the association for the production of wealth may satisfy justice?

(i)   it must be entered freely

(ii) there must be no payments without services.

(iii) the control and interpretation of the terms of association must be in the hands not of powerful individuals, but of an authority commanding general confidence.

(iv) the canon 'payment according to services' must be modified so as to prohibit payments which, even if greater than services, are incompatible with the dignity of man not as a worker but as a man. I.E. the *first* charge must be the maintenance of a decent human life.

27 February. The question of our day is by what *right* is the control of industry vested in the hands of those who control it today? To the ordinary workman his economic status is determined by *compulsion*, not by choice. What he desires is to determine it by choice not by compulsion. The former is slavery: the latter is freedom.

But, it will be said, the economic life of mankind always has been settled by compulsion, the compulsion to labour. This is one of those dangerous ambiguities which deceive even the elect. The truth is this. Over the greater part of Western Europe at any rate down to the end of the 17th century, the plain man had the choice of (a) work at wages (b) work on the land as a squatter. It was not true therefore that he was at the mercy of compulsion applied by any human agency. He could always escape from it. That, of course was realized by the governing classes. What else is the meaning of praedial serfdom and of maximum wage legislation except *this*, that the employer knows that the worker is not at his mercy, and that if squeezed too hard he will cease being employed at all, and employ himself?

This idea is certainly historically true. The moral of it is that the economic subordination of one class to another by the mere absence of alternatives to wage labour is a modern phenomenon and creates quite a new moral and economic problem, viz. the problem of securing liberty *within* the industrial system now that the opportunity of securing liberty by *leaving* the industrial system has been taken away. No one bothered about the sovereignty of Parliament till the central government had drawn the whole nation into its net. Then they made a revolution to assert that men are governed by *consent*

not by *force*. No one bothered about industrial sovereignty as
long as the individual could escape from the industrial system.
Now that all men are imprisoned for good and evil within it,
freedom must be found in the same way.

13 June. (I): 'Cooper had a funny end: became an evangelical
preacher.' (BEER).[1] 'I am surprised at nothing which happens
to those who have been through the moral crisis of a revolution.
I have myself.'

16 June. What I mean by society needing a philosophy is this.
No machinery, whether of the state or minor corporation, can
apply ideas which do not exist in society. They must always
act at second hand. They must always be fed from without. All
that a statute can do is to reduce a philosophy (important or
trivial) into sections which are sufficiently clear to be under-
stood even by lawyers. Hence the great days of a Parliament
are when there is outside Parliament and in society a general
body of ideas which Parlt. can apply. It has no *creative force*.
There *is* no creative force outside the ideas which control men
in their ordinary actions. There is no *deus ex machina* who can
be invoked though men are always trying to discover one. Nor
is the modern futility of Parliament due to mechanical difficulties, which can be removed by mechanical remedies, such as
revolution. It is due to the absence of any general accepted
philosophy of life. Our principal task is to create one.

[1] Max Beer, author of *A History of British Socialism* (1920), to which Tawney
added a preface. The reference is probably to the Chartist leader and poet,
Thomas Cooper.

29 June. The rise of the capitalist = the poodle in Faust turning into the devil. The Parliamentary Labour Movement = the devil turning into the poodle.

30 June. The true history of St Paul: He was offered a Professorship at Athens, which he accepted, and became a distinguished writer on the New Morality, the Conflict between Science and Religion, and the substantial identity between Greek Philosophy and Christian Thought.

12 July. If H. were writing of religion now, he would not speak of the night in which all cows are black,[1] but of the gaslight in which all creeds are relatively white.

People who turn from Christianity to some kind of personal, naturalistic, semi-mystical religion, do so under the impression that the essential characteristics of Christianity are common to all creeds, and that they are merely discarding the crudities which were inseparable from the 'historical conditions' in which Christianity arose. They believe themselves to be dropping accidents of time and place, and that in proportion as the conditions of the first century of a partially Romanized,

---

[1] Walter Kaufmann, in his *Hegel. Reinterpretation, texts, and commentary* (1965), p. 386, offers this translation of the relevant passage in the Preface to the *Phenomenology of Mind*: 'To pit this one piece of information, that in the absolute all is one, against all the distinctions of knowledge, both attained knowledge and the search and demand for knowledge – or to pass off one's absolute as the night in which, as one says, all cows are black – that is the naïveté of the emptiness of knowledge.' It is possible that Tawney varied Hegel's aphorism slightly, since he probably attended C. Delisle Burns's lecture on the philosophy of Hegel which was delivered on 18 August 1911 to a W.E.A. audience at Oxford. The title of the lecture was 'The Night in Which All Cats Look Black'. (Cf. University Extension Oxford Summer Meeting, 1911, *Report of Proceedings* (1911), pp. 25–6).

partially Graecized, oriental province are expunged, they rise to the large philosophical air where all sensible and kindly men agree.

I have been, and I suppose, am, on this road myself, and I believe it leads nowhere. Where those who take this view err is that they forget that a religion must be judged, as a man or a book or a society must be judged, by what is individual, characteristic, and peculiar to itself not merely by what it has in common with all or most reasonable men. Now it is, of course, perfectly true that we do not need Christianity to make us aware that God exists. That fact, in my view, is a fact of experience, by which I mean that consciousness of contact with a personality, or with a source of thought and emotion, is a fact of direct experience infinitely more immediate than reflection on an absent but existing person, and analogous to the consciousness of the presence of a person in the same room as oneself, whom one is not a[t] the moment looking at, and with whom one communicates nonetheless easily on that account. But this is a commonplace. The special new and characteristic contribution of Christianity – its differentia – is the statement that God became, or was fully expressed in, a particular historical individual as to whose life we possess records. The significance of this is immense. What it tells is not merely that God exists – which we knew already – but that the God who exists is like Christ. That is to say, it shows God not as universal, but as individual, not as infinite, but as limited and defined, not as a principle but as a man. I can easily conceive a person thinking this untrue. But I cannot conceive his thinking it unimportant. One may be driven to 'natural religion' as a *pis aller*. But no one but a fool would *choose* it in preference to Christianity. A man who *prefers* the absolute to the Trinity is like a man who would voluntarily abandon his house and wander in a desert. How many, alas! have to do so.

What I mean is this. I think that the knowledge that God exists is a source of immense strength to man. But it is not by itself very helpful. What we want to know is what kind of God he is, and what he is like in ordinary human intercourse. This is what Christianity tells us.

9 August. It is evident that the fundamental questions of social policy in the future are going to turn very largely on the relation between societies and the state. No one now believes in pure individualism. Few are contented with pure collectivism. Hence the rise of various proposals for escaping the former without appealing to the latter. Syndicalism, gild socialism etc.

How state management deadens spiritual life is evidenced by the Church of England. How syndicalist management fosters corporate selfishness is shown by the bar and by Oxford and Cambridge.

November. 'Men of science are like children gathering pebbles on the beach,' and they usually throw them at one another.

November. The present tendency of all writing on social and economic subjects is to collect vast accumulations of facts. But what is the use of them when they are collected? No amount of conjuring will turn a fact into a principle.

November. Some writers point to the striking development of

municipal services in the last thirty years as an indication of the triumph of 'socialism'. This is an awful example of the worship of the letter and the neglect of the spirit. The *motive* of nearly all these developments has been a purely utilitarian consideration for the consumer. They have not been inspired by any desire to introduce juster social arrangements, nor, in particular, by any consideration for the wage-earner. They have been inspired simply by the desire for cheap services akin to the free trade agitation. In fact the two movements appealed to much the same classes. Manchester manufacturers want cheap gas and electricity for exactly the same reason that they want cheap cotton and machinery. Clearly there are no germs of a revolution here.

November. The working classes and the English Labour Movement have made one tragic mistake. They have aimed at *comfort*, instead of aiming at getting their *rights*, including the right to do their duty. The contest is therefore being fought out on a low plane, and the attack can be bought off by instalments of 'social reform'. It has become not a question of right and wrong, but a question of more and less.

29 November. If I ever have the chance I want to write books on the following subjects
  (i)   The Social and Economic History of the French Revolution, including economic thought.
  (ii) The Social and Economic History of the English Reformation.
  (iii) The rise of capitalism, beginning with the end of the 16th century, describing the economic policy of the Tudors and first 2 Stuarts, the economic causes for the

opposition of the middle classes to the monarchy, the growth of the sects, the economic ideas of the Levellers, Diggers, ending with the economic results of the Revolution of 1688.

But shall I ever *have* time?

2 December. As an illustration of the way in which fundamentals are neglected, take the question of unemployment. First we had relief for the unemployed, then insurance for the unemployed, then schemes of training. But no one has asked 'By what right does A, who owns a factory, dismiss and/or hire B, his partner who works in the factory?' But this is, of course, precisely the fundamental question. What I should propose is that A should not have the legal right to dismiss B, without due process of law, that B should have an appeal to a court or Representative Committee against A; in short that B shall be given a legal interest in his job, a tenant-right. The analogy to the land question is instructive. Doles were given to relieve those evicted in Ireland, but it was the recognition of the three Fs, followed by land purchase which made the peasants prosperous instead of poor. With my proposal compare the policy of gilds down to the 17th century, which regard the 'right to a job' as a fundamental principle. I have not worked out the details, but what I have in mind is that when an employer gives a workman notice, the workman may, if he please, appeal to a Court of Referees of some kind, who may compel the employer to withdraw it.

28 December. If one takes a broad view of the nature of this war, and ceases the futile discussion 'who began it?' one sees

that to a considerable extent [it] is the natural outcome of the ideals and standards which govern Western Europe, especially Germany and England, in its ordinary every day social and economic life. I do not mean that this is a 'capitalists war', though to some extent it is. I mean that our whole tendency is to exalt the combative qualities, and to undervalue those of the humble and meek, and that the existing economic organization of society is a perpetual evidence that the world gives its applause to energy, pugnacity, ruthlessness. The existing social order is Macchiavellian [*sic*], in the sense of rewarding successful and unscrupulous cunning. It is inhuman in the sense of using men as means – 'hands' – not as ends. It is pagan, in its exaltation of strength, its contemptuous crushing of the weak, its disbelief in the value of human beings *qua* human beings. The scale of values which horrifies us when it appears in the claim of some Prussians to have a right to determine the future of 'weaker' or 'inferior' nations, which identifies right with power, and recognizes no obligation which cannot be enforced on them by superior force, that conception of human affairs is only to similar to that which a cool observer would consider to be realized in our industrial system. Of course we do not, as individuals accept this, and shld deny it with horror if taxed with it. But social traditions, institutions, and practices grind on and draw us into cooperating with the machine in spite of our subjective feelings. Modern industry has no body of ethical doctrine to control our crude instinct to believe that success is its own justification. The types which it carries to power tend to be not unlike those produced by war. They must have energy, self-control, foresight, a willingness to take risks. They must be undisturbed by pity for the weak, by doubts as to

the value of the immediate ends at which they aim, by reverence
for the finer and more delicate human qualities and
achievements, by humility or consciousness of personal
deficiencies. They are essentially a conquering race. Like
other conquerors, they confer great benefits which are usually
no part of their design: system and organization, order,
facilities for accumulating vast material resources, power to
conquer natural obstacles, a field for splendid careers for the
bold, the energetic, the unscrupulous. Like other conquerors
they leave a trail of wreckage, consisting of the weak, the
exceptionally scrupulous and honourable, the unconventional,
the merely gentle and kindly who 'dare not have the lives of
others on their conscience'. So I say again: war is not the
reversal of the habits and ideals we cultivate in peace. It is their
concentration by a whole nation with all resources on an end as
to which a whole nation can agree. As long as mankind believe
that the normal order of society should be one in which the
strong win their way to power over the ruin of the weak, so long
will it find nothing fundamentally abhorrent in the
intensification of that struggle to the point at which 'peace'
ceases and 'war' begins. If we are to end the horrors of war, we
must first end the horror of peace. There are no mechanical
arrangements by which men who regard society as a struggle for
existence can be prevented from fighting. There is one way and
one only: to abandon the standards of good and bad, success
and failure which are expressed in the existing arrangements of
industry, property, and social life, and to seek to make society,
when it is at peace, a field in which mere power, ruthlessness,
ambition, can *not* override the merciful and gentle.

INDEX

References to Tawney's views are italicized

84